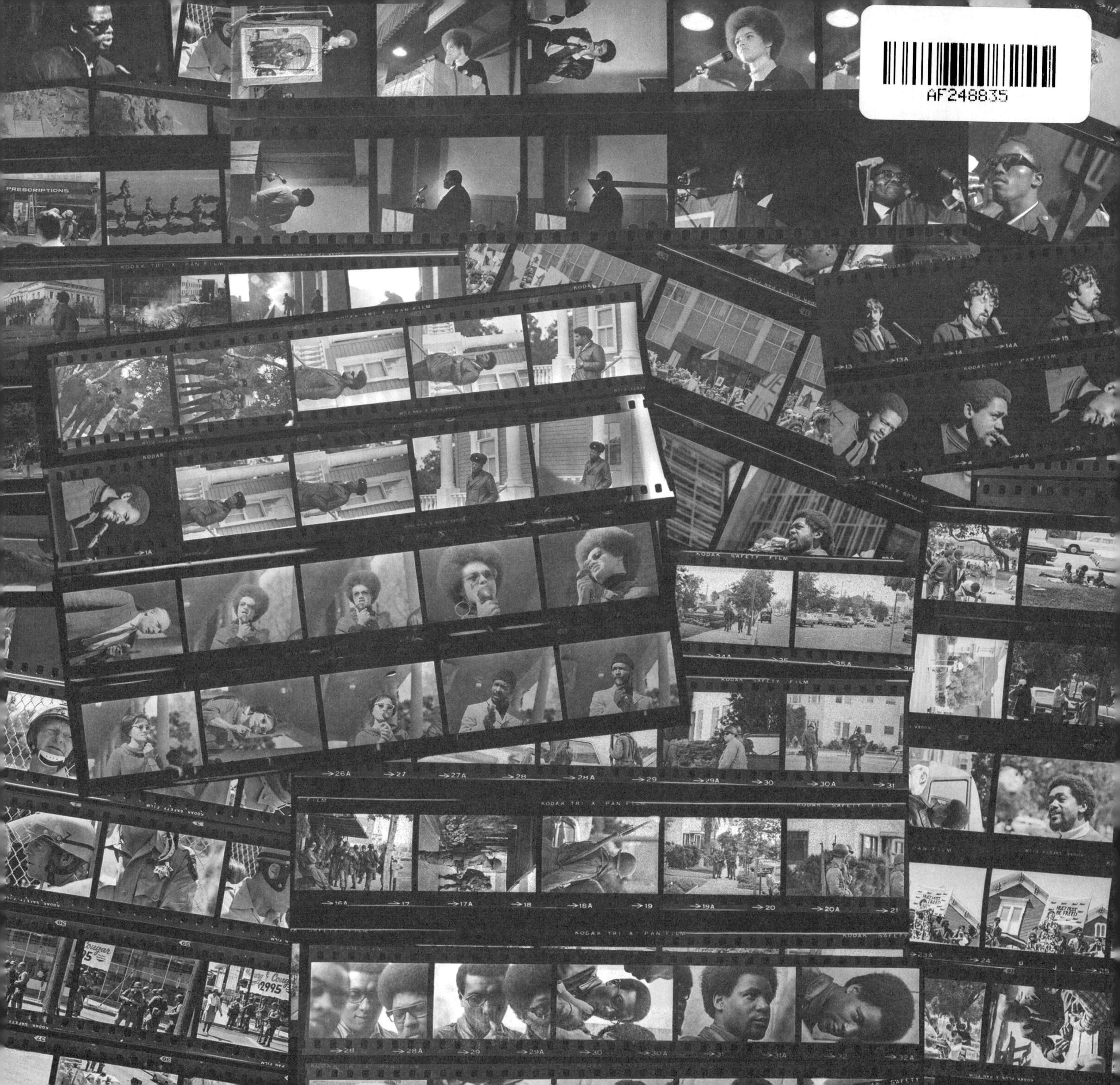
AF248835

# IN A TIME OF PANTHERS

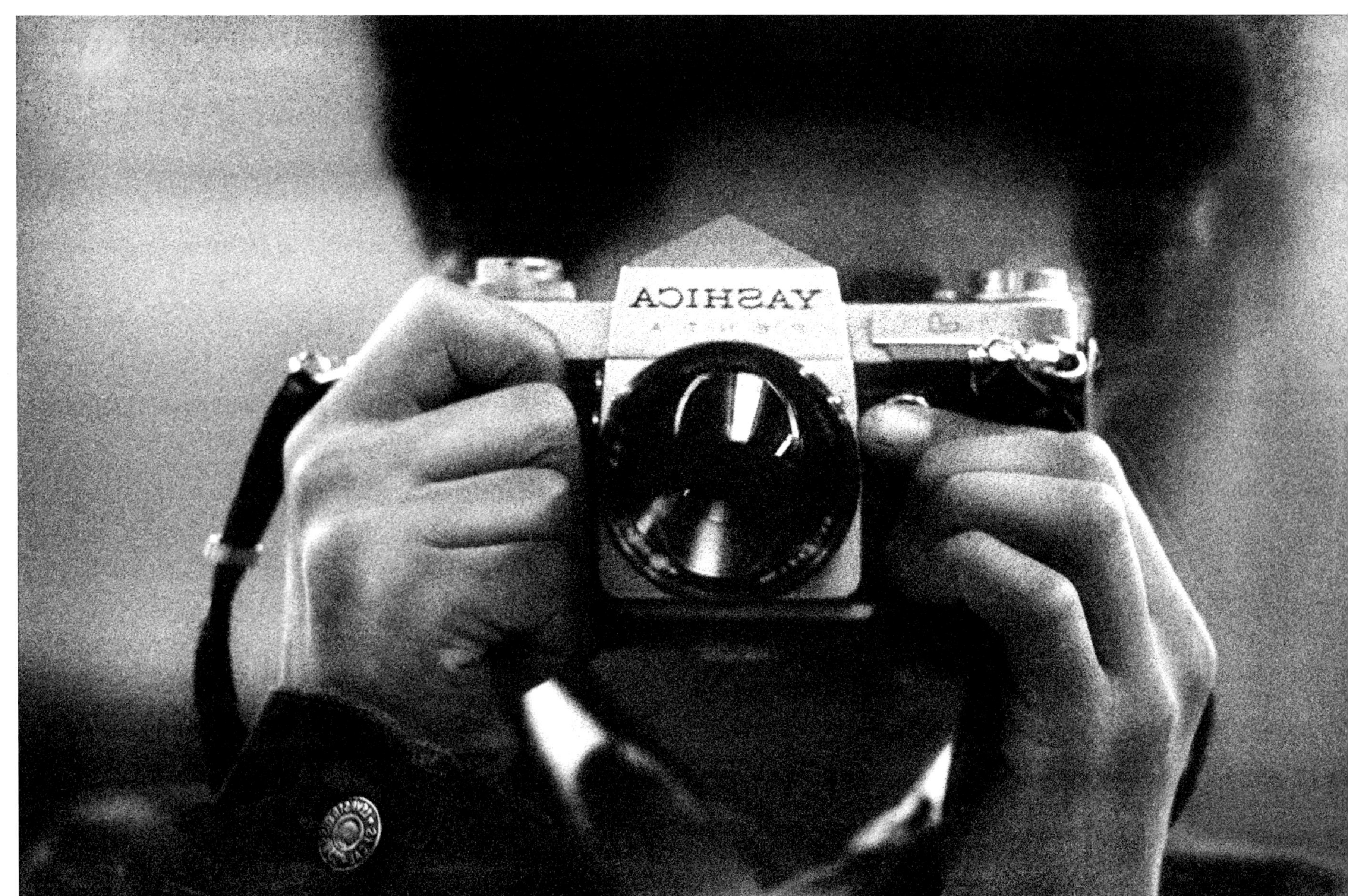
YASHICA

# IN A TIME OF PANTHERS

## EARLY PHOTOGRAPHS BY JEFFREY HENSON SCALES

SPQR EDITIONS · BROOKLYN, NY

# PHOTOGRAPHING THE REVOLUTION:
## JEFFREY HENSON SCALES AND THE
## BLACK PANTHER PARTY

## BY DEBORAH WILLIS

*The revolution will not be televised*
*Will not be televised*
*Will not be televised*
*Will not be televised*
*The revolution will be no re-run, brothers*
*The revolution will be live[1]*
*- Gil Scott-Heron*

*Stand!*
*In the end you'll still be you*
*One that's done all the things you set out to do*
*Stand*
*There's a cross for you to bear*
*Things to go through if you're going anywhere[2]*
*- Sly and the Family Stone*

I FRAME THIS ESSAY WITH THE WORDS OF Sylvester Stewart and Gil Scott-Heron because they help us imagine a time in the 20th century when these photographs were created, a time that helped to name, and to visualize, the black experience. Growing up in North Philadelphia and studying photography when the Black Panther Party was organizing safe spaces in communities around the country, I remember the breadth of their initiatives, from free breakfast programs and study groups to the free medical clinics housed in vacant storefronts near Temple University. On the other side of the country, in Oakland, Califor-

---

[1] Gil Scott-Heron, *The Revolution Will Not Be Televised*, ©Carlin America Inc., 1971.
[2] Sylvester Stewart, *Stand!*, 1969. © (Renewed) Mijac Music. All rights on behalf of Mijac Music administered by Warner-Tamerlane Publishing Corp. (BMI).

nia, a teenaged Jeffrey Henson Scales turned his attention to documenting activism on the West Coast with a camera his father gave him. My father also gave me a Brownie at an early age, and we spent many hours turning the pages of picture magazines like Life, Look, National Geographic and Ebony—just as the young Scales did with his dad. Although we did not know it at the time, Scales and I were part of a nationwide movement. All over the country, young people witnessing injustices started to organize and protest. Many of them picked up their cameras to process the pain, discontent, and joy of the moment, documenting a live revolution, answering the clarion call to Stand!

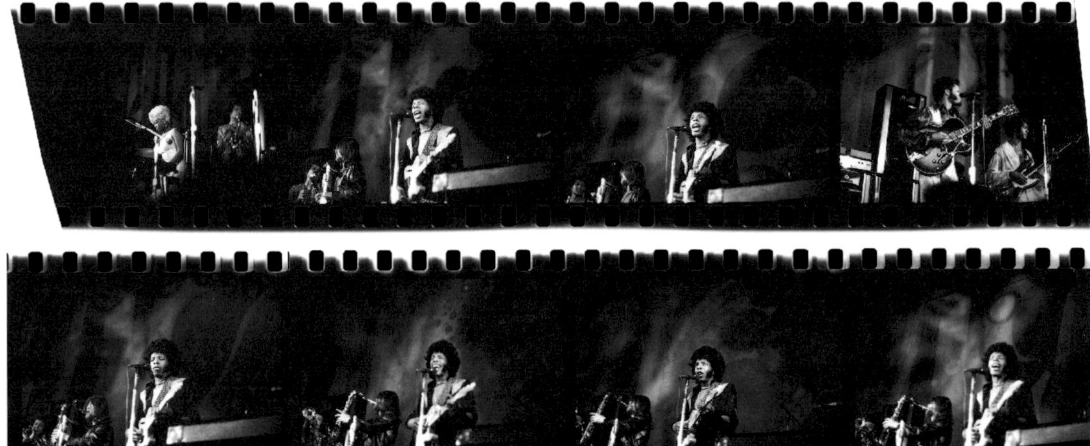

Sly and the Family Stone, Winterland Ballroom, San Francisco, 1969.

The images depict an era when a multitude of social movements were indicating discontent with a political order that was rooted in racial inequality. The era also is manifested by the presence of the memory of this time in our hearts, minds, and actions today. These photographs also shape our personal and collective memories of this time. In the 1960s, this nation experienced a proliferation of events that changed our understanding of injustice, illuminating events like the Vietnam War and Anti-War Movement, the Civil Rights Movement, Black Arts Movement, Black Panther Party, and the Black Power Movement. The 1960s proved to be the culmination of an era of youth-driven resistance. Two landmark events make this point clear: On April 4, 1968, Dr. Martin Luther King Jr. was shot and killed in Memphis, Tennessee, leading to protests in Washington, DC, Boston, Detroit, Kansas City, Los Angeles, and other major cities. One week later, President Lyndon B. Johnson signed the Civil Rights Act of 1968, on April 11.

Music was a prolific form of protest that captured the fervor of the time. Many artists, singers, activists, and musicians used their fame and exposure to speak out against injustice. Aretha Franklin told the world to "Think." The Rascals insisted that "People Got to Be Free." Sly and the Family Stone called for everyone to "Stand!," and James Brown urged people to "Say It Loud, I'm Black and I'm Proud." Mark Anthony Neal writes that "Black music has long been thought of as a balm for Black trauma in the United States, to the point that there is a certain expectation that what Black musicians choose to produce should easily map onto the political realities of the time."[3]  By placing these issues within a new book on images of the Panthers, Scales guides us through a period that transformed the political climate of the United States. Just as black music was the balm for black trauma, Scales' images help us to understand the diversity and complexity of the 1960s and the people who lived through those years, never looking away from the trauma, rage, and brutality, but also looking at the beauty, community, joy, and the fight for citizenry.

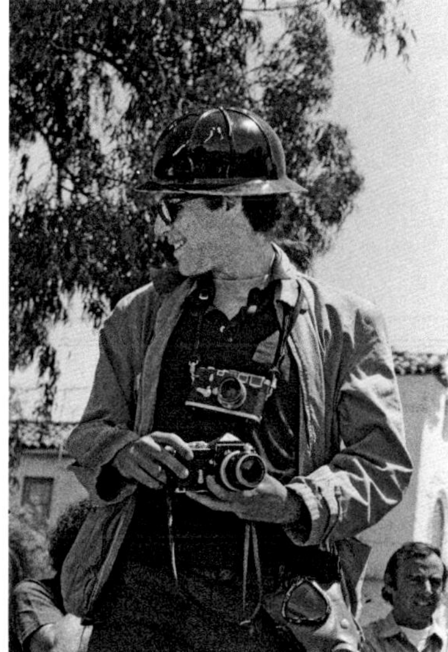
Stephen Shames, 1969.

Like Scales, activists Huey P. Newton and Bobby Seale were residents of Oakland in 1966. They formed the Black Panther Party for Self-Defense after witnessing systematic abuse of power by police, politicians, landlords, and business owners in their city. Newton, Seale, and other Panthers vehemently challenged human and civil rights abuses in Oakland, encouraged by the voting rights and desegregation activities of civil rights organizations like the Student Nonviolent Coordinating Committee (SNCC) and the Lowndes County Freedom Organization (LCFO). The LCFO's banner included an image of a black panther, a symbol of strength, freedom, determination, and beauty. As Seale recounted:

> Most of our ideas were similar to those of other civil rights organizations at the time—full employment, decent housing, education that taught African Americans their true history, an end to the exploitation of our black community, preventive health care, fair trials, and the enforcement of our constitutional rights....[4]

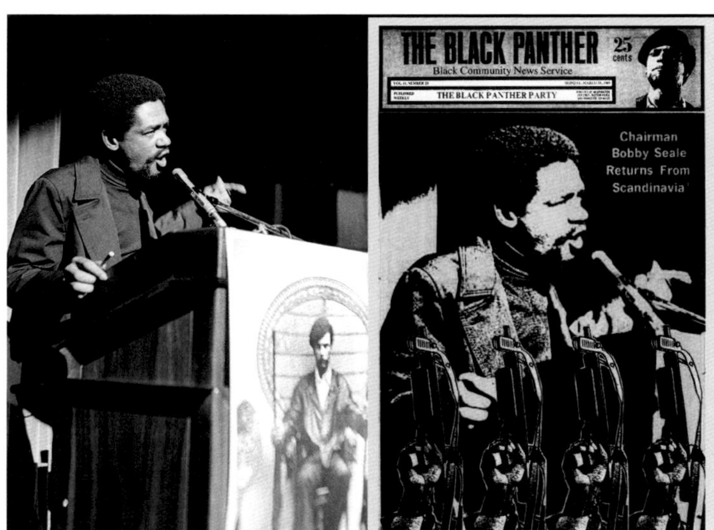

One of Scales' photographs of Bobby Seale on the cover of The Black Panther newspaper.

3 Mark Anthony Neal, 1968: Soul Music and the Year of Black Power, Black Perspectives, December 31, 2018; https://www.aaihs.org/1968-soul-music-and-the-year-of-black-power/.

4 Bobby Seale, Foreword, The Black Panthers: Photographs by Stephen Shames (New York: Aperture Foundation, 2006), p. 11.

The images in this book showcase exactly what Seale described. Through a series of captured moments, Scales photographed Seale speaking at podiums and assessing the mood of the crowd. One image that exemplifies the urgency of the time shows Seale with a cigarette in his right hand as he gestures with his left. His spotlit face reveals the intensity of the moment.

In addition to Seale and Newton, Scales was exposed to a variety of political leaders, photographers, artists, and activists, including Stokely Carmichael (Kwame Ture), Eldridge Cleaver, and photojournalist Stephen Shames. Mentored by Shames and Panther members and influenced by Life and other magazines his father shared with him, Scales developed a vision and a passion for visual storytelling. Looking to create a powerful image, whether with a Kodak Instamatic or a 35mm, he considered the politics of black beauty, dignity, fashion, and identity. In some of his images that highlighted the inequality and inequity in the areas he photographed, he positioned his camera at unique angles. For example, in Chicago in 1967 he photographed what appears to be a police arrest in progress (page 21). Looking off a balcony, he captured three young men facing a wall; one has his hands folded across his stomach, while the two are either kneeling or in the act of kneeling. The urban sidewalk bordered by grass is cluttered with discarded paper; a uniformed police officer stands nearby.

He captured a small group of Panthers along with a stylishly dressed couple waiting at a Free Huey rally at DeFremery Park in Oakland (page 42). The woman wears a straw hat, large sunglasses, a polka-dot tie, and a white blouse. The suited man, also wearing sunglasses, is wearing a hat known as a brim; he looks directly into Scales' camera lens.

The park is where Scales captured a range of distinctively impressive photographs, including Seale standing on a raised platform, looking away from the camera as he appears to make a strong point in his speech by accentuating the issue with his raised index finger (page 44).

In September of '68, Scales photographed Panther supporters standing on a sidewalk across from the Alameda County Courhouse in Oakland as the Huey P. Newton trial was being held (pages 32-33). They were holding posters showing Newton seated in a rattan chair, wearing a beret and a black leather jacket while holding a shotgun in his right hand and a spear in his left hand. Scales reads this provocative scene well, offering the viewer an opportunity to imagine the tenseness of the time.

It's hard to believe that this stunning archive preserving the work of a young emerging photographer was lost for some 40 years. As Scales describes it, family members discovered the negatives in a large file cabinet in 2018 after the death of his mother. Take a minute to think about the foresight of his mother in deciding to save an archive of her young activist son's photographs and negatives—what could be considered vital records for the authorities—in a metal file for safekeeping. Scales recalled, "I always assumed it was stolen by the

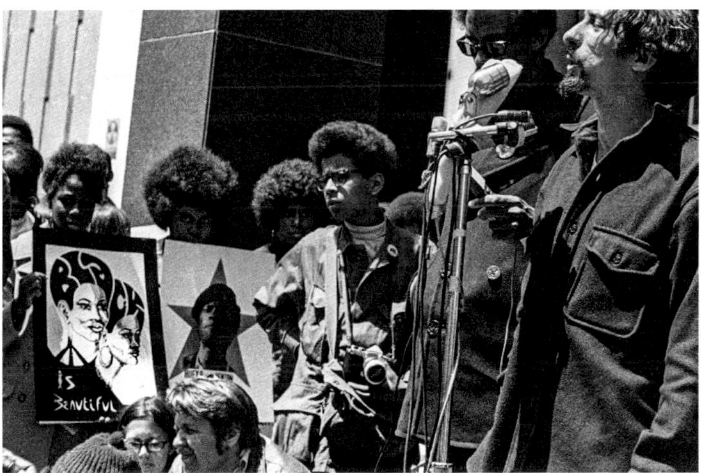

14-year-old Jeffrey Henson Scales at a May Day Free Huey rally in San Francisco, 1969. Photograph by Janine Wiedel.

FBI.... At the time, it wasn't an unfeasible assumption because my family was under surveillance by the FBI. They looked like they were in *The Matrix*, sitting in unmarked cars parked in front of our house and making movies of us."[5]

This singular belief of the artist that the "lost negatives" were in the hands of the FBI punctuates the anxiety that I imagine Scales' mother must have experienced. Clearly she understood that his work would have value for future generations. It provides insight into the mind of an activist's parent and her understanding of the necessity of the work, which is both rare and profound as an iteration of a lineage of activism. And Scales' photographs reveal his desire to interpret local activi-

ties that had the potential to change the world. Scales says:

> I hadn't seen these images since the 1960s until recently and was struck by not only my origin story as a photographer but also the new urgency these images and the civil rights movement takes on in the context of today's ongoing struggle for racial justice....These images serve as a time capsule of sorts, not only of my adolescence and political awakening, but also for a country whose struggle with racial inequality, police brutality and resistance is as urgent and timely as ever.

In looking at these works today, I see a young photographer who was questioning and challenging the images of party members presented by the press. It is evident that Scales was aware that he was living in a time when young people were calling for a change, and he was there to do the same with his camera. What makes his photograph of Stokely Carmichael (later Kwame Ture) waiting on the steps of the courthouse (page 30) so compelling is the way in which Scales captured the face of a young outspoken civil rights leader with such reverence that the viewer feels seated right next to him, listening to the people chatting in the crowd. There is a sense of hope because of his presence in Oakland.

Indeed, there is a sonic experience in looking at these photographs. One can almost hear the voices of the speakers, the call-and-response moments of the supporters, and the words of the protest songs and chants.

5 Miss Rosen, *Rediscovering Historic Photos of the Black Panther Party in 1960s Oakland*, Blind Magazine, Photography at First Sight, October 11, 2021.

These images capture their subjects in unguarded moments. Through the lens of the young Scales, we encounter Huey P. Newton seated at his press conference following his release from prison on August 5, 1970 (page 101).

We meet Eldridge Cleaver, Minister of Information, and other party members outside the Alameda County Courthouse in 1968 (page 38). They all wear the signature Panther uniform of black leather jackets, Panther pin-back buttons, and black berets.

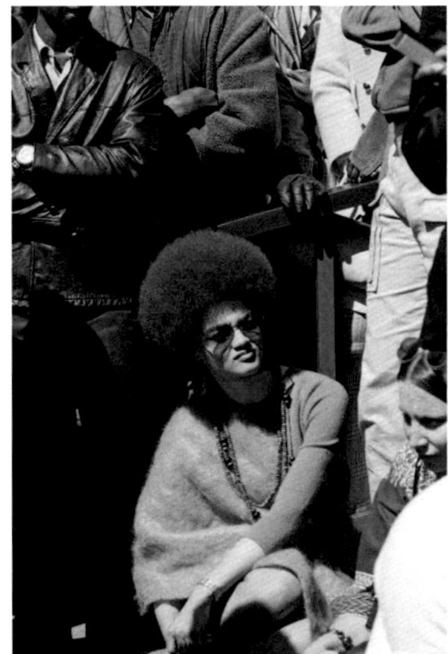

Kathleen Cleaver, 1969.

We see Kathleen Cleaver in 1969 wearing a light-colored mohair shawl, sitting on steps at a rally in San Francisco (page 78). She and the crowd listen to the speaker while Scales directs his lens toward Ms. Cleaver's revolutionary style—Afro, hoop earrings, beads, and sunglasses.

Other images are both striking and haunting. Scales powerfully presents the death of 17-year-old Panther member Bobby Hutton through abstraction. "Lil' Bobby" was the party's first casualty. His death hit a black community still reeling from the assassination of Dr. Martin Luther King Jr. just two days earlier. As historian Ashley Farmer points out, "Newton's arrest, Hutton's murder, and King's assassination became the triumvirate of events that tipped the scales of popular opinion toward the Panthers' brand of insurgency.[6] It's difficult to look at the bullet holes in the wall. While they clearly mark the violent death of Hutton, with the absence of his visage the viewer is left with the awful memory of his horrific killing at the hands of police. Community and Panther members staging protests around the country could have used this photograph to pressure the media and government officials into changing the status quo. Scales' images, whether in street scenes or impromptu portraits, situate us in a time and stir our emotions in a way that only photography can do (pages 34, 35 & 37).

This book introduces us to a young visionary who eventually would spend his entire career illustrating how impactful photography can be. Along the way, Scales has served as an editor, professor, and mentor. His documentary photographs have been exhibited throughout the United States and Europe and have appeared in numerous publications, including the monograph House, in which he documented a single Harlem barbershop over five years. His photographs are in the permanent collections of the Museum of Modern Art, the Museum of Fine Arts, Houston, the City Museum of New York, the George Eastman House, the Minneapolis Institute of Art, the Weisman Museum of Art, the Indianapolis Museum of Art at Newfields and the Baltimore Museum of Art.

§

---

6 Ashley D. Farmer, *Remaking Black Power: How Black Women Transformed an Era*, (The University of North Carolina Press, 2017), p. 67.

DEBORAH WILLIS is University Professor and Chair of the Department of Photography & Imaging at the Tisch School of the Arts at New York University and has an affiliated appointment with the College of Arts and Sciences, Department of Social & Cultural Analysis, and Africana Studies. She received a MacArthur Fellowship and a Guggenheim Fellowship and is a member of the American Academy of Arts and Sciences. Willis is the author of *The Black Civil War Soldier: A Visual History of Conflict and Citizenship; Posing Beauty: African American Images from the 1890s to the Present; Out [o] Fashion Photography: Embracing Beauty; Reflections in Black: A History of Black Photographers — 1840 to the Present; Let Your Motto be Resistance — African American Portraits; Family History Memory: Photographs by Deborah Willis; VANDER-ZEE: The Portraits of James VanDerZee.* She is a co-author of *The Black Female Body: A Photographic History,* with Carla Williams; and the NAACP Image Award winning books *Envisioning Emancipation: Black Americans and the End of Slavery,* with Barbara Krauthamer; and *Michelle Obama: The First Lady in Photographs,* with Emily Bernard.

# YOUNG, GIFTED, AND BLACK

## BY WALDO E. MARTIN JR.

IN THE LATE 1960S AND EARLY 1970S, a surprising number of people thought The Revolution was just around the corner. Particularly in the San Francisco Bay Area, revolutionary change seemed not just possible, but also imminent. For an influential minority, revolutionary consciousness and action increasingly overshadowed reformism. In this transformative time, the electrifying Oakland-based Black Panther Party for Self-Defense took center stage. Founded in late 1966 by Bobby Seale and Huey P. Newton, the party epitomized this galvanizing revolutionism, which went in multiple national and international directions and in turn found an amazing array of adherents and expressions. Indeed, these intersecting, parallel, and divergent expressions of revolutionism inevitably influenced one another.

As Seale noted at the time, the Panthers seized this ripe historical moment and indelibly helped to shape it. The party's fundamental belief in "All Power to the People" showcased a profound understanding of the crying need for ordinary folks, especially regular Black folks everywhere, to take control of their destinies and fight for progressive change.

The Black Panther Party almost immediately became the most important political expression of the Black Power phase (1966-1980) of the Black freedom struggle, one of the most consequential social movements of the twentieth century. Precisely because of its urgency and gathering strength, the Black Power insurgency soon overshadowed the enduring Civil Rights phase of that broader freedom struggle.

Jeffrey Henson Scales' youthful and extraordinary photographic explorations of the early Black Panther Party as well as political struggles in Berkeley and Oakland in the late 1960s and early 1970s vividly capture ordinary individuals attempting, and often achieving, extraordinary things. These struggles, successes, and, sometimes, failures are a defining theme of the movements for Black Power and Civil Rights as well as concurrent social movements like Women's Rights, Gay and Lesbian Rights, and Disability Rights.

Scales was an idealistic, middle-class Black teenager coming of age in this intoxicating moment. Two successful mass movements convulsed his world as a Berkeley high school student. First, the party's brilliant campaign to "Free Huey," jailed for allegedly killing a policeman, expanded the party's reach and influence. Second, militant local protests led to the creation of People's Park (a few blocks from the University of California campus). Like the "Free Huey" campaign, the making of People's Park was another tangible, symbolic, and powerful example of grassroots insurgency. These sensational movements clearly captivated Scales.

The era's cross-fertilizing movements defined this heady time. For the highly inquisitive and sensitive young Scales, the Panthers anchored that complex and at times chaotic moment. It helped solidify his growing sense of purpose and belonging, as the party adopted him and his evolving and talented photographic eye for the party's cultural work. What we see in these striking photographs, viewed collectively, is a revealing intertwined autobiographical sojourn and a historically specific place, time, and movement.

Scales' revealing window onto that remarkable time enables us to better see the party's essence. It was fundamentally a youth-student movement. The awe-some contemporary beauty, energy, magnetism, and profound hopefulness of Black youth-student activism in particular catch the eye. Many of these photographs vividly illustrate what it meant at that Black Power moment, in the words of Black playwright-activist Lorraine Hansberry — words crafted into a stirring anthem by her friend Nina Simone, the "High Priestess of Soul" — "To Be Young, Gifted, and Black."

In addition, the aesthetic and hypnotic as well as intense political power of Blackness — of the "Black Is Beautiful" cultural politics of the time — dazzle. These photos graphically evoke this rich and evolving consciousness. They exude the moment's ubiquitous emphasis on Black pride. They resonate passionately with the incomparable Godfather of Soul James Brown's sonic invocation: "Say It Loud — I'm Black and I'm Proud."

Similarly, these photos compellingly illuminate African American struggles over complicated issues of individual and collective identity. To return to an enduring question: Who are we? In the late nineteenth century, W.E.B. Du Bois offered a classic formulation: "One feels his two-ness, — an American, a Negro; two souls, two thoughts, two unreconciled strivings; two warring ideals in one dark body, whose dogged strength alone keeps it from being torn asunder. The history of the American Negro is the history of this strife, — this longing to attain self-conscious manhood, to merge his double self into a better and truer self."

Flash forward to the late 1960s and early 1970s, the height of the Black Power Movement. At this particular moment in the broad sweep of the African American historical journey, from slavery to freedom, what did it mean to be "Black," rather than, say, "Negro," or "Colored"? Put another way, what did Blackness mean in this specific historical context? At this time, in this place — situated within a white supremacist world — how did we as Blacks affirm Blackness as positive (rather than negative)?

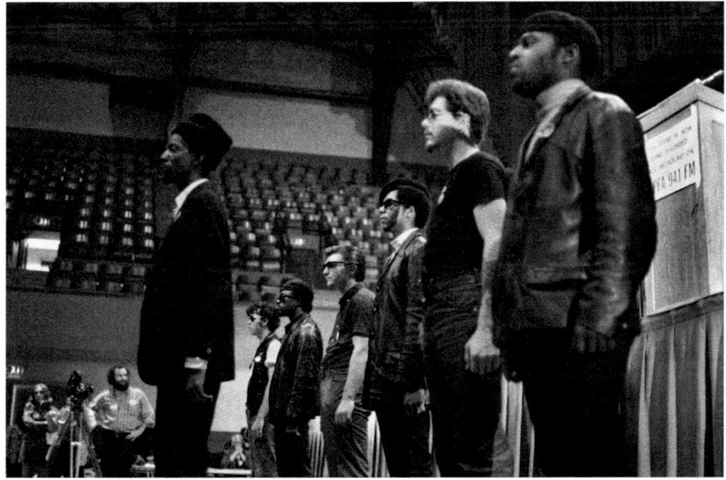

Members of the Illinois Young Patriots alongside Panther members providing security at The United Front Against Fascism conference in 1969.

For one thing, as these photographs so vividly illustrate, beautiful and empowering images of Blackness matter profoundly. Such images help shape how we see ourselves, our world, our present, past, and future. Positive, affirmative, and in fact, quite complex expressions of Black identification course throughout. Such images are absolutely essential to the continuing war, waged on the battlefront of visuality, to affirm and empower Blackness — to advance it as a means toward achieving a universal humanism, a common humanity — and, in tandem, abolish white supremacy.

While centered on the struggle for Black freedom, the Black Panther Party's politics were fundamentally humanist and anti-racist. The party's revolutionary Black Nationalism was Black-based yet inclusive; it was neither Black separatist nor racially exclusive.

That inspiring commitment to egalitarian humanism can be seen in the striking images of Black-led interracial mobilizations, including Asian Americans, Latino Americans, and Native Americans as well as white Americans fighting to "Free Huey." It can be seen in the cross-racial alliances of those who attended the party's 1969 "Revolutionary Conference for a United Front Against Fascism." That pioneering conference in turn led to a network of National Committees to Combat Fascism. These efforts linked the struggles of the oppressed in the U.S. to freedom struggles around the world.

Seen another way, the party was pro-human: anti-racist, not anti-white. Interracial, multiracial, and cross-movement mass mobilizations — notably large rallies featuring the wide range of people of color and whites who supported the party — strikingly capture its humanist politics. While the party's membership was largely Black, its broad ranks of supporters, allies, fellow travelers, and hangers-on constituted a rainbow coalition.

These visual documents, then, help us to better see America's enduring struggles over national identity politics. To reposition an earlier question: Who are we? What and who is an American? How do we as Americans see and represent ourselves as a nation and as a people? As noted above, for African Americans — as a Black nation within a predominantly white nation — these questions have always been fundamental to struggles over identity, over issues of self-definition and self-determination.

We also see the local geography of the Black freedom struggle, beginning with the very first photographs that Scales ever took: Chicago street scenes shot during the Long Hot Summer of 1967, when there were riots over racial injustice in many cities across the country. These remarkable photographs evoke Black inner-city areas throughout the U.S., including Oakland. There we witness scenes of the Alameda County Courthouse and DeFremery Park, sites of innumerable party-led rallies

Bullet holes in West Oakland home where Panther Bobby Hutton was killed by Oakland police after a shootout on April 6, 1968.

and mobilizations to "Free Huey." The images of the struggle for Black freedom and the jarring scenes of the violent battles between the police state and Berkeley activists over People's Park, in which the U.C. Berkeley campus became a war zone, are sobering.

Especially sobering, indeed chilling, are the photographs taken by a 14-year-old Scales of the bullet-riddled walls of the house where 17-year-old Bobby Hutton, the party's first recruit, stripped down to his underwear with his hands in the air, was murdered by the police (pages 34, 35 & 36). This murder on April 6, 1969, two days after the assassination of Dr. Martin Luther King Jr., clearly seared Scales, who took his photographs of the murder scene the very next day. The long history of the racist state's galling, violent, all too often murderous mistreatment of Black men particularly and Black people generally comes through loud and clear.

In search of his own understanding of what it meant to be a young Black man coming of age in the Black Power era, Scales deeply identified with Hutton. A striking graffiti-style painting of Hutton, Scales' first artwork for the party, graced the cover of The Black Panther, the party's newspaper. Reflective of this focus on Black masculinity, many of the most fascinating photographs feature very serious young Black men taking care of party business and witnessing party events. Equally riveting and revealing are the photographs of Black women, including leaders like Kathleen Cleaver, Elaine Brown, Marsha Taylor and protesting rank-and-file members.

The beautiful, mesmerizing faces. The infectious seriousness of purpose. The compelling politics, dress, style, "swag." Above all else, a deep-seated and undying love for the people, for Black people — a love central to the party's politics and history — shines brilliantly here. Ultimately rooted in the Black quest for both self- and collective Black love, the party exemplified love for all humanity. In this long-gone revolutionary moment, the party asked not just Blacks, but everyone, what it meant, in the words of Roberta Flack and Donny Hathaway, to "Be Real Black for Me."

§

WALDO E. MARTIN JR., the Alexander F. and May T. Morrison Professor of American History and Citizenship at the University of California, Berkeley, is the author of *No Coward Soldiers: Black Cultural Politics in Postwar America* (2005), as well as *Brown v. Board of Education: A Short History With Documents* (2021) and *The Mind of Frederick Douglass* (1985). He is a co-author, with Mia Bay and Deborah Gray White, of *Freedom on My Mind: A History of African Americans, With Documents* (2021) and, with Joshua Bloom, of *Black Against Empire: The History and Politics of the Black Panther Party* (2016). With Patricia A. Sullivan he co-edited *Civil Rights in the United States: An Encyclopedia* (2000). Aspects of the modern African American freedom struggle and the history of modern social movements unite his current research and writing interests. He is completing *A Change Is Gonna Come: The Cultural Politics of the Black Freedom Struggle and the Making of Modern America.*

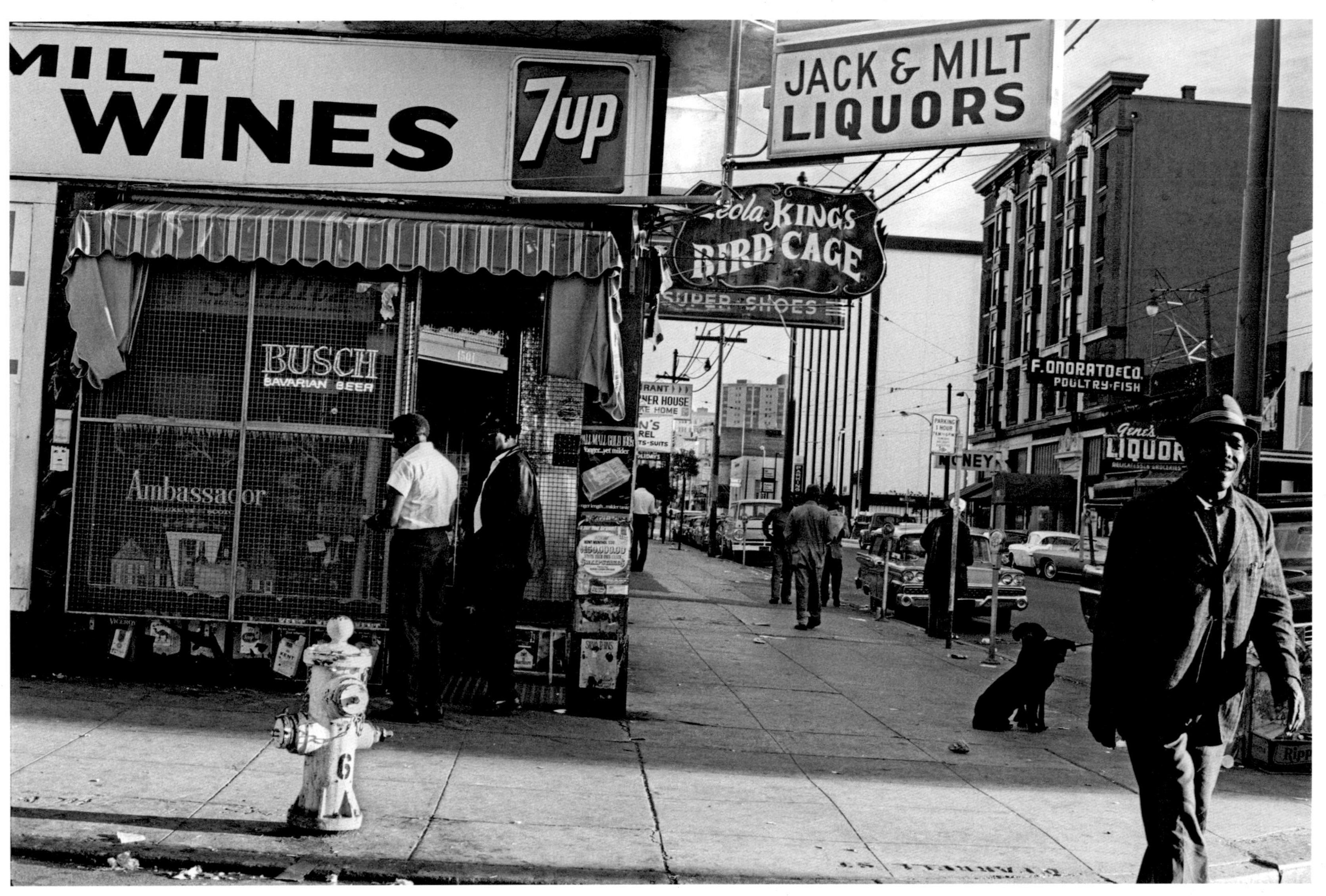


Fillmore and O'Farrell Streets, not far from the San Francisco Panther National Distribution office, and the legendary nightclub, Leola King's Bird Cage.

In 1967 on a trip to Chicago, my
grandmother gave me a Kodak Instamatic
camera so that I could pursue
what then was just a hobby.

On this humble Instamatic I created my first
social documentary photos. One of those
rolls was part of the collection my mother
filed away.

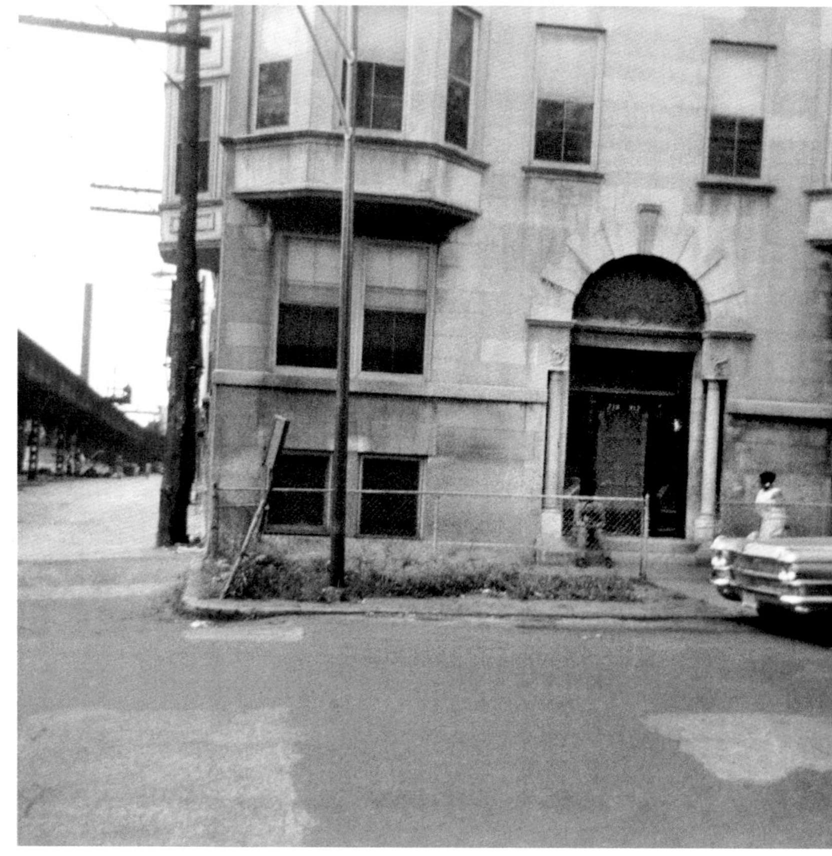

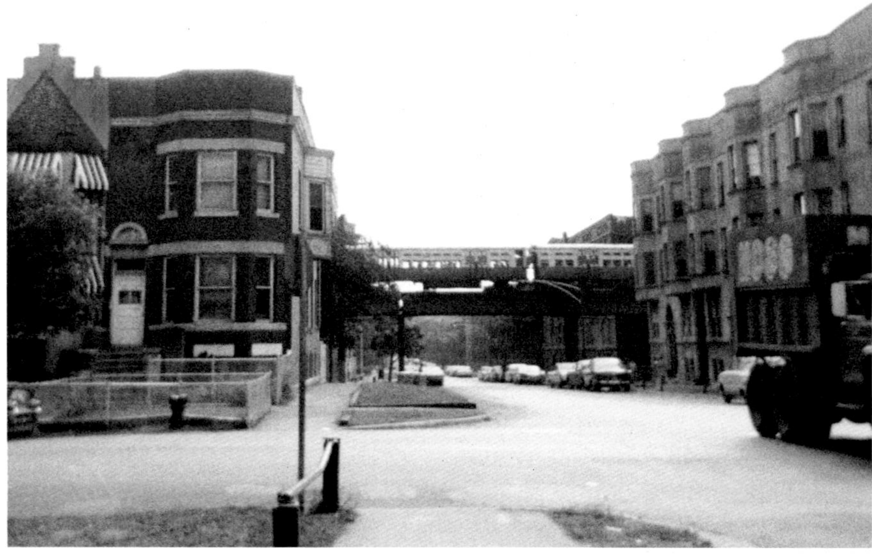

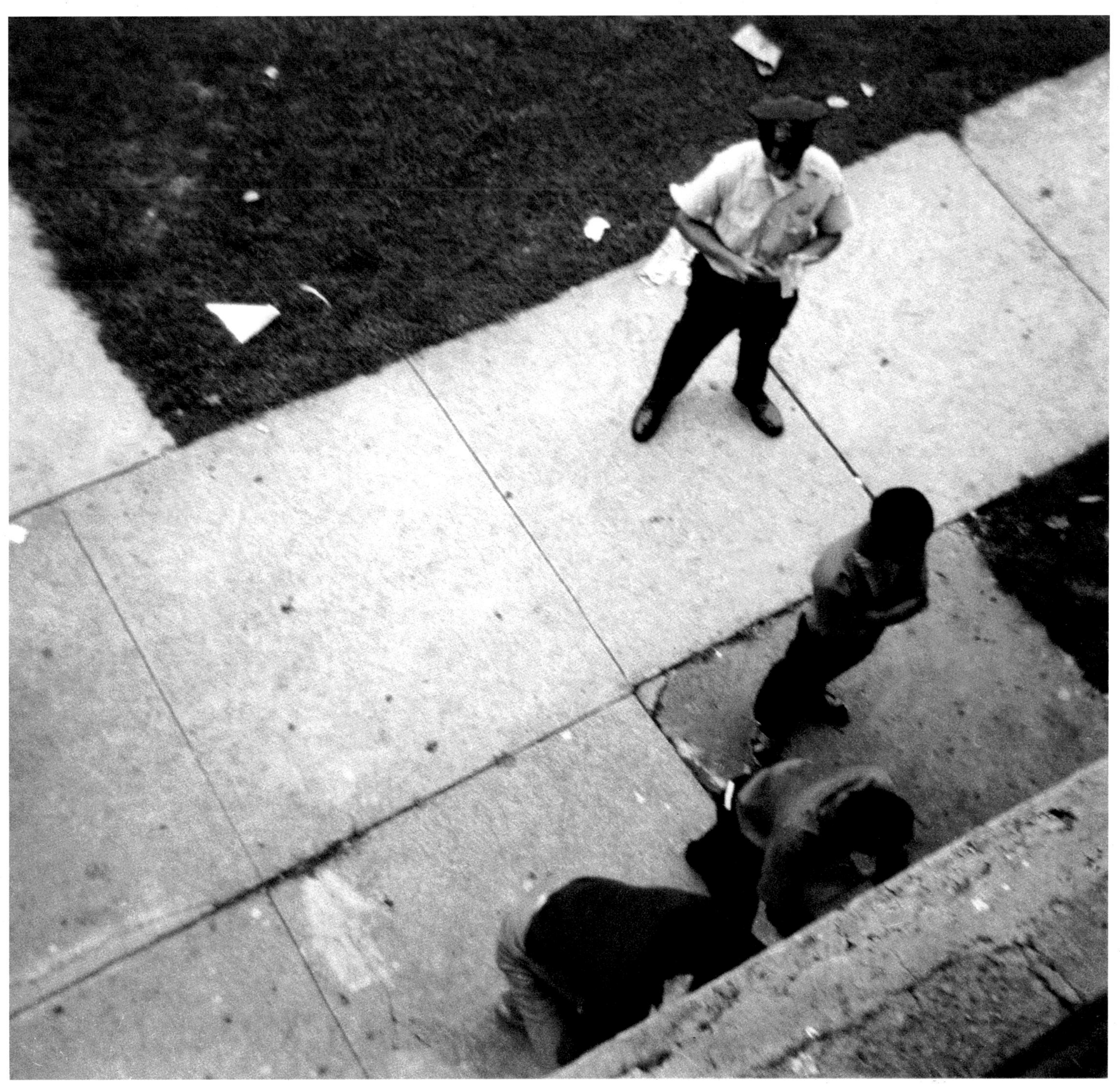

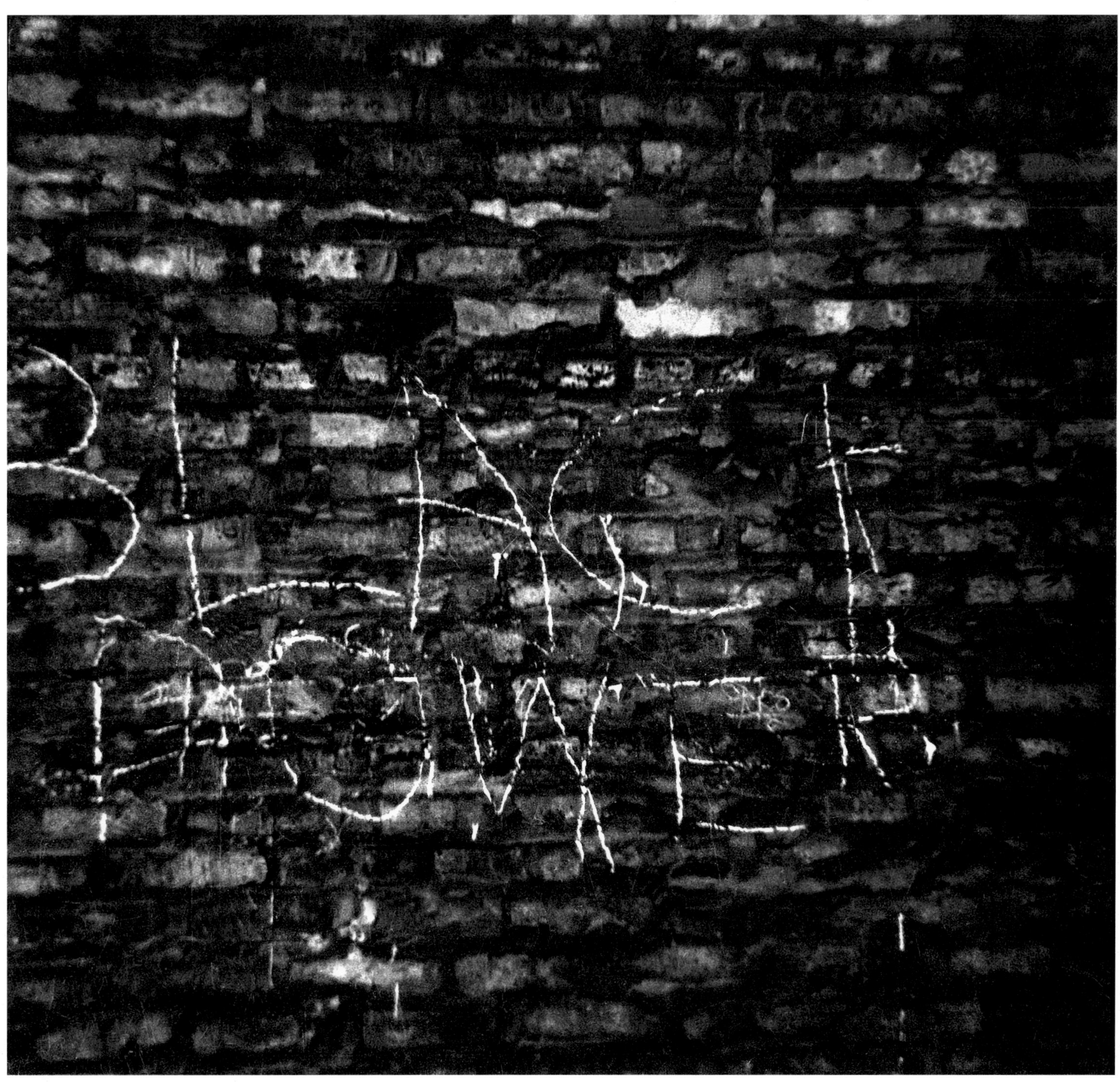

Graffiti, Chicago, 1967.

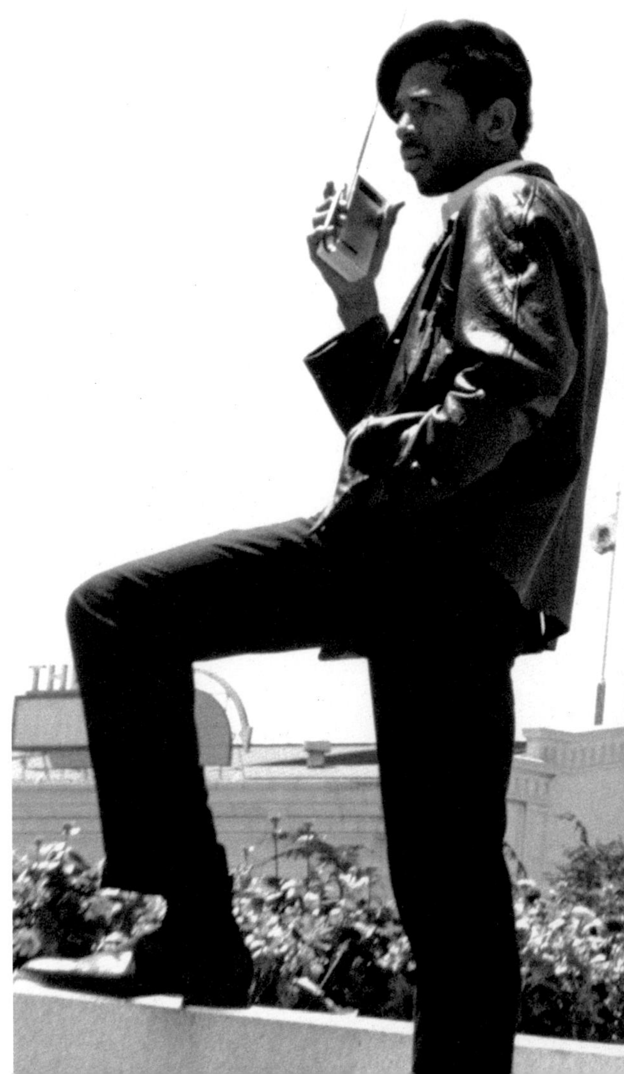

From left: Panthers Van Taylor, John Boweman and Richard Brown
outside the Alameda County Courthouse, 1968.

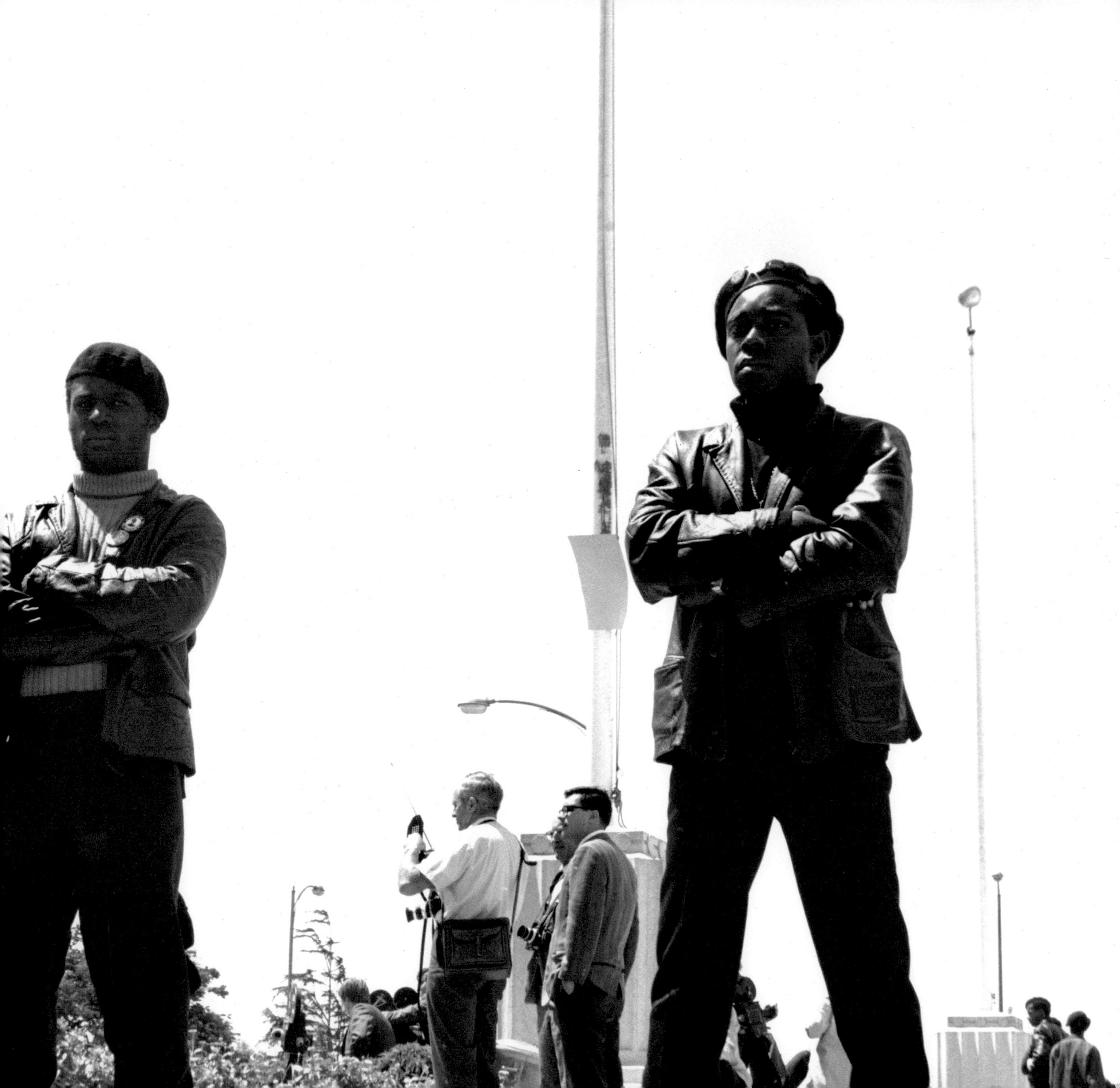

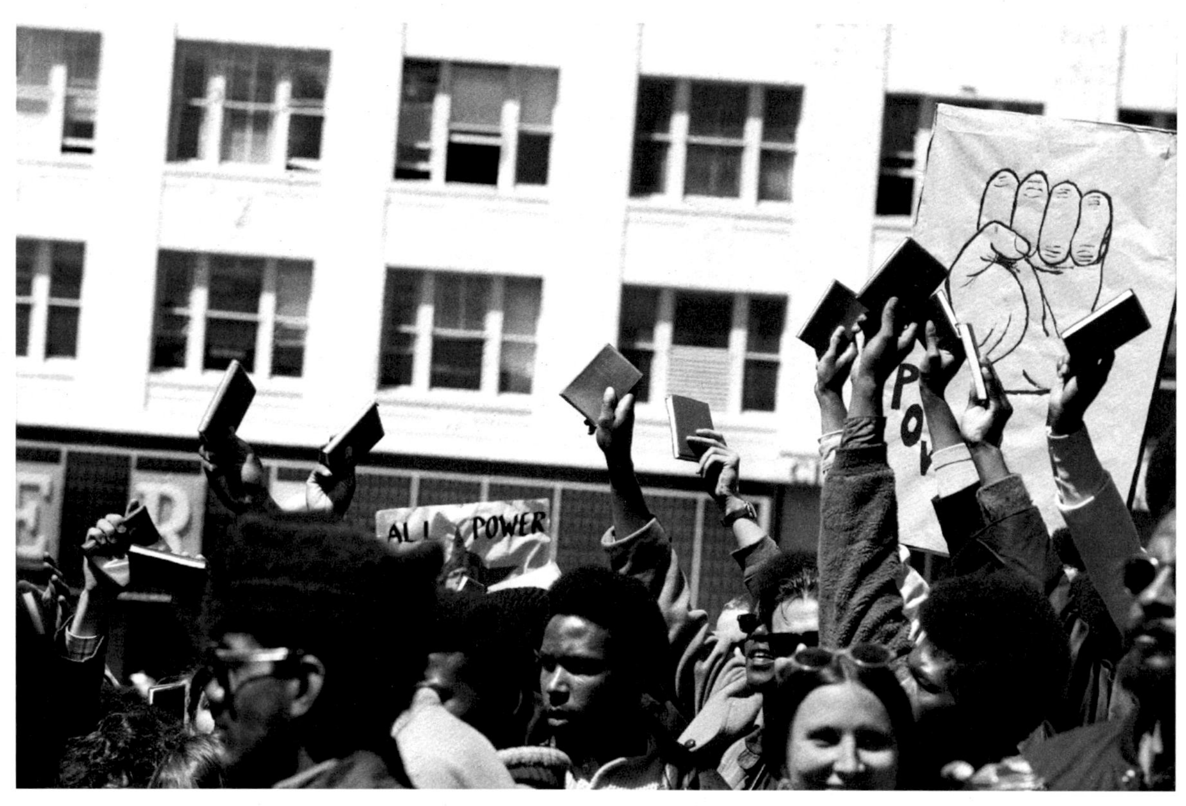


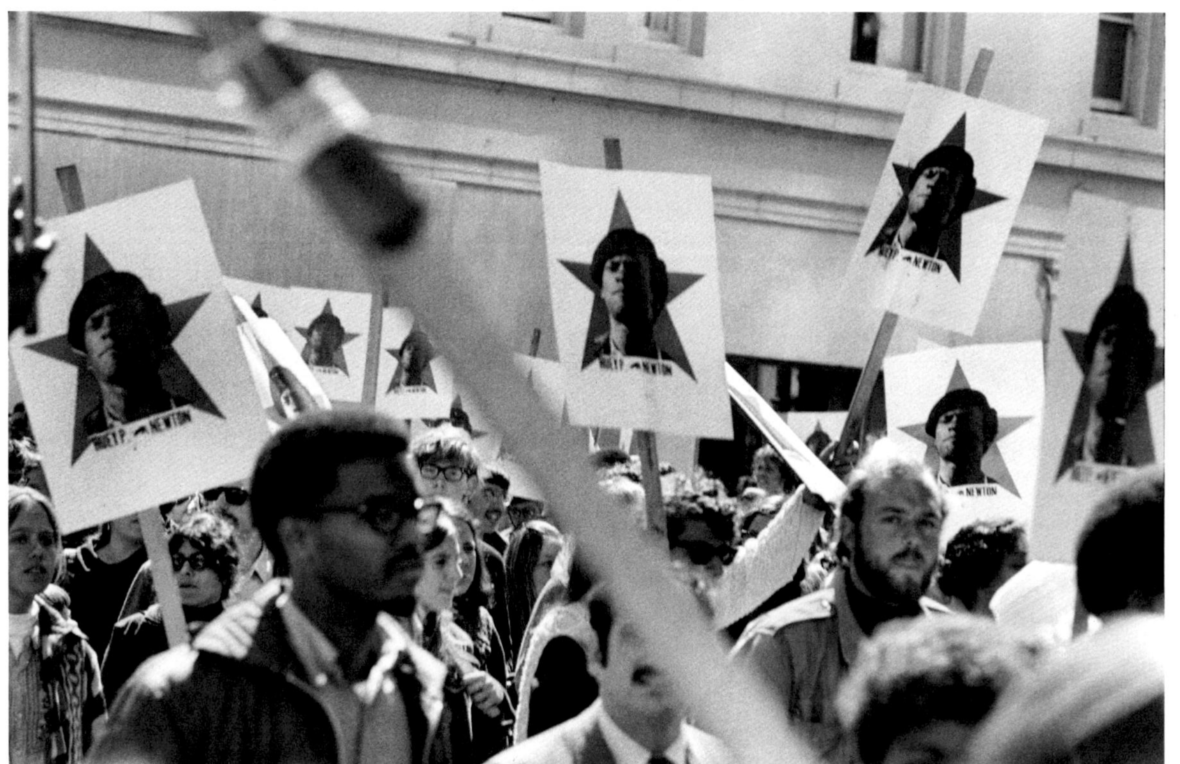


May Day rally to free Huey P. Newton
the Federal Building in San Francisco,
May 1, 1969.

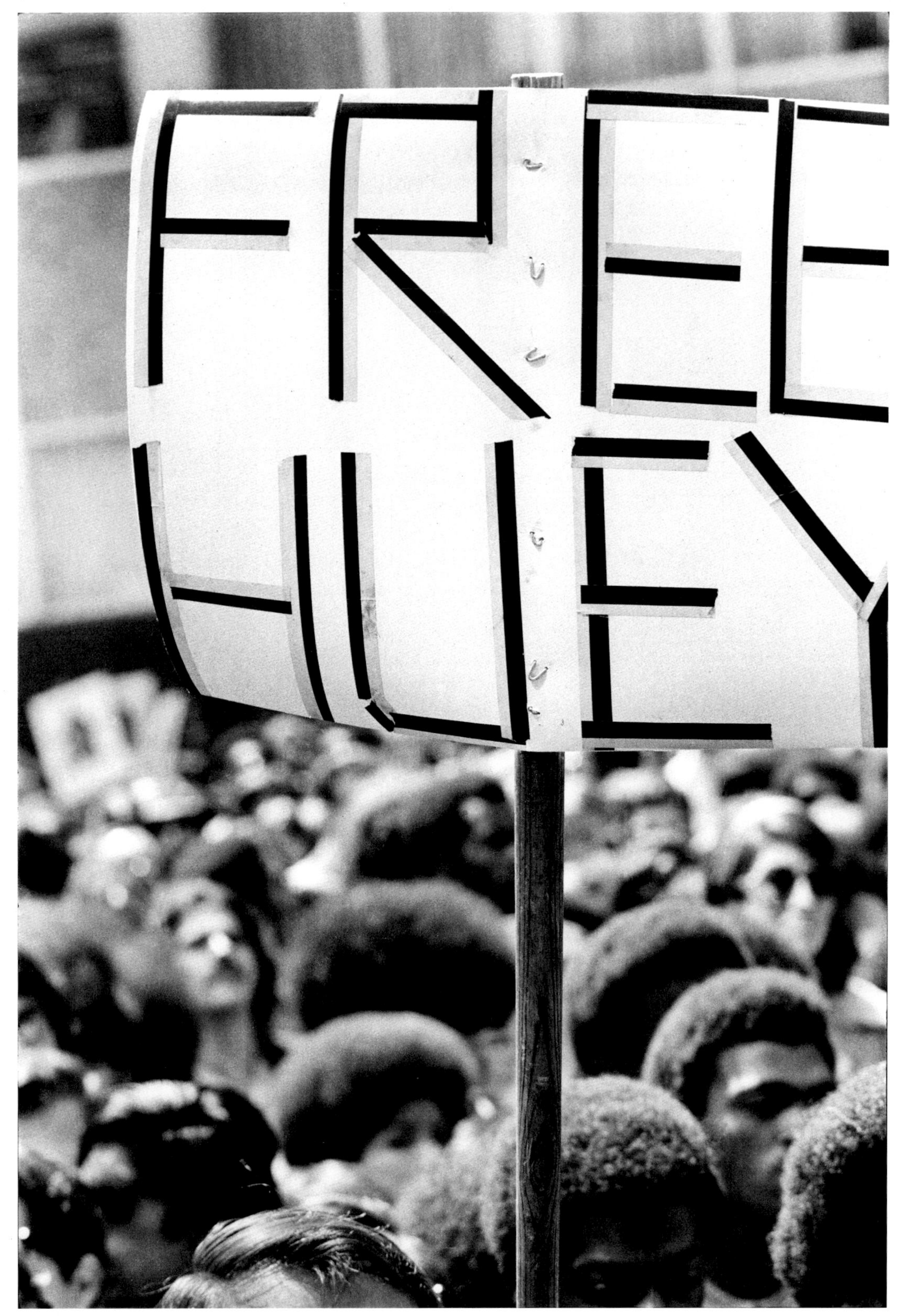

FREE
HUEY

For a 14-year-old just out of the eighth grade, the summer of 1968 couldn't have been a better time for the Huey Newton trial. When I would hear about events or photo-ops from the Panther leadership, or from photographers like Stephen Shames and Pirkle Jones, I was always available. Many days I would get up early and go to the trial, which lasted from July 15 to September 8. The whole world was watching, and so was I. Although I could watch, no cameras were allowed in the courtroom.

The Alameda County Courthouse, an 11-story granite and concrete WPA Moderne structure, fills an entire square block, just opposite Oakland's Lake Merritt. That summer and fall, the Panthers often held demonstrations or simply maintained a highly visible presence there during the trial.

It was a remarkable trial. To attend, you had to get to the courthouse around 6 or 7 A.M. and wait in line. Sometimes it was quiet, with just a few people, and I'd get a good seat. But there were days when it was so much more. One morning Stokely Carmichael was there; I had the good fortune to be in line near him as well as Eldridge and Kathleen Cleaver, Emory Douglas, Donald "DC" Cox and others. We all had to wait, then be hand searched by Alameda County sheriff's officers. Bobby Seale used to say that because I was a kid and they wouldn't scrutinize me so much, I should get a small camera and conceal it on my body so that I could photograph in the courtroom on the DL. I never tried, but I always appreciated the idea of going that far to take a photograph.

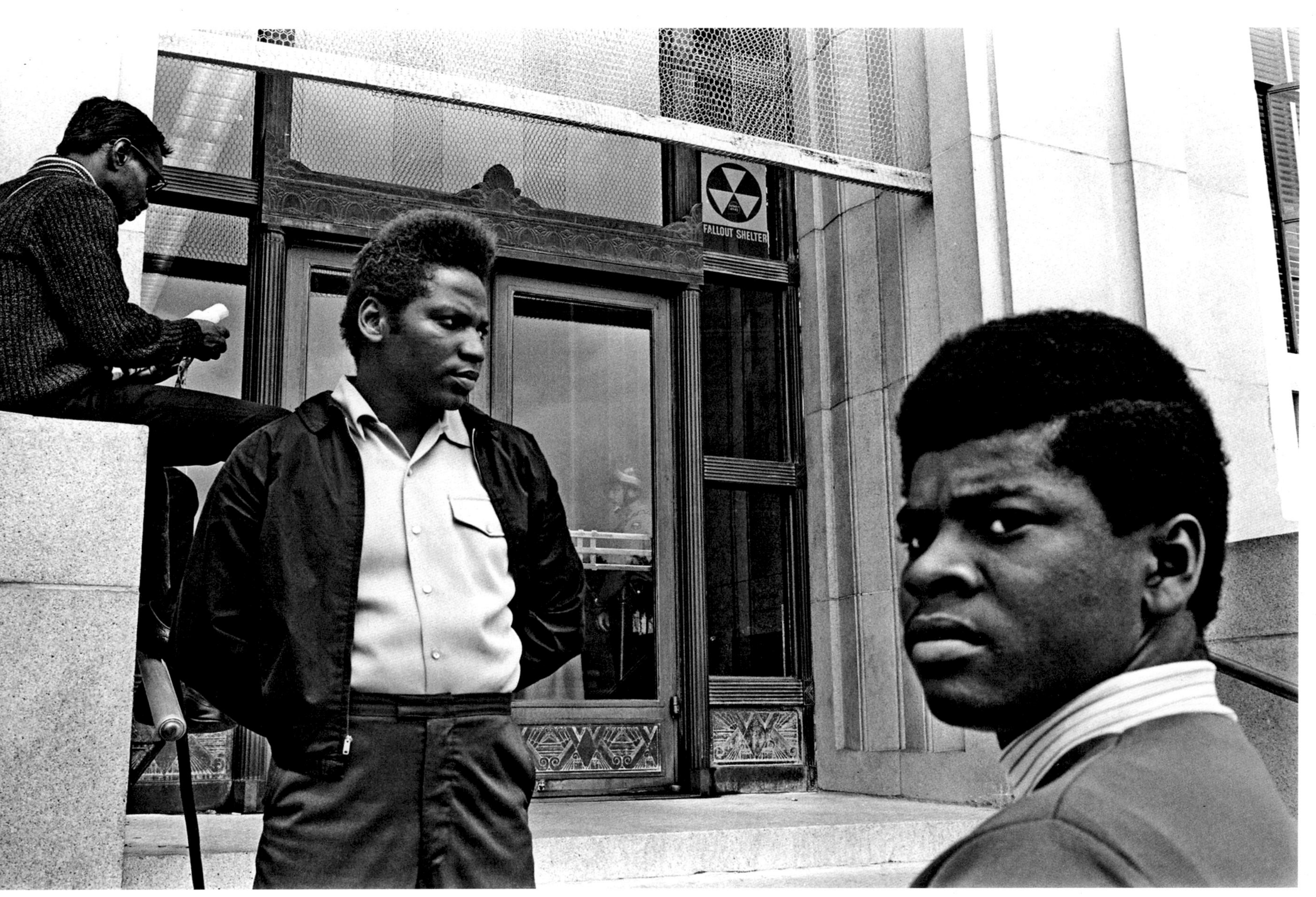FALLOUT SHELTER

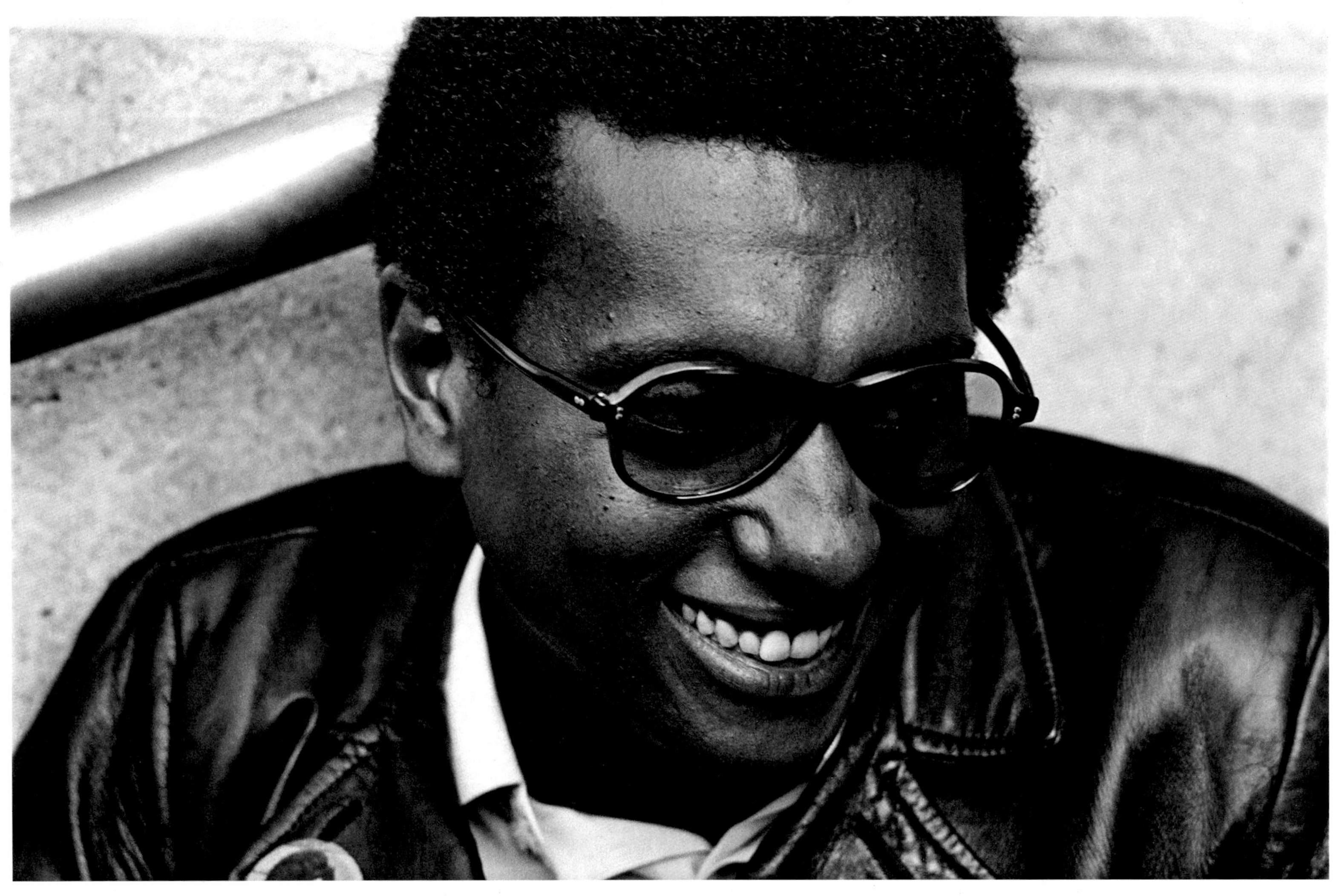

Stokely Carmichael, aka Kwame Ture, waiting outside the Alameda County Courthouse
to attend the trial of Huey P. Newton in 1968.

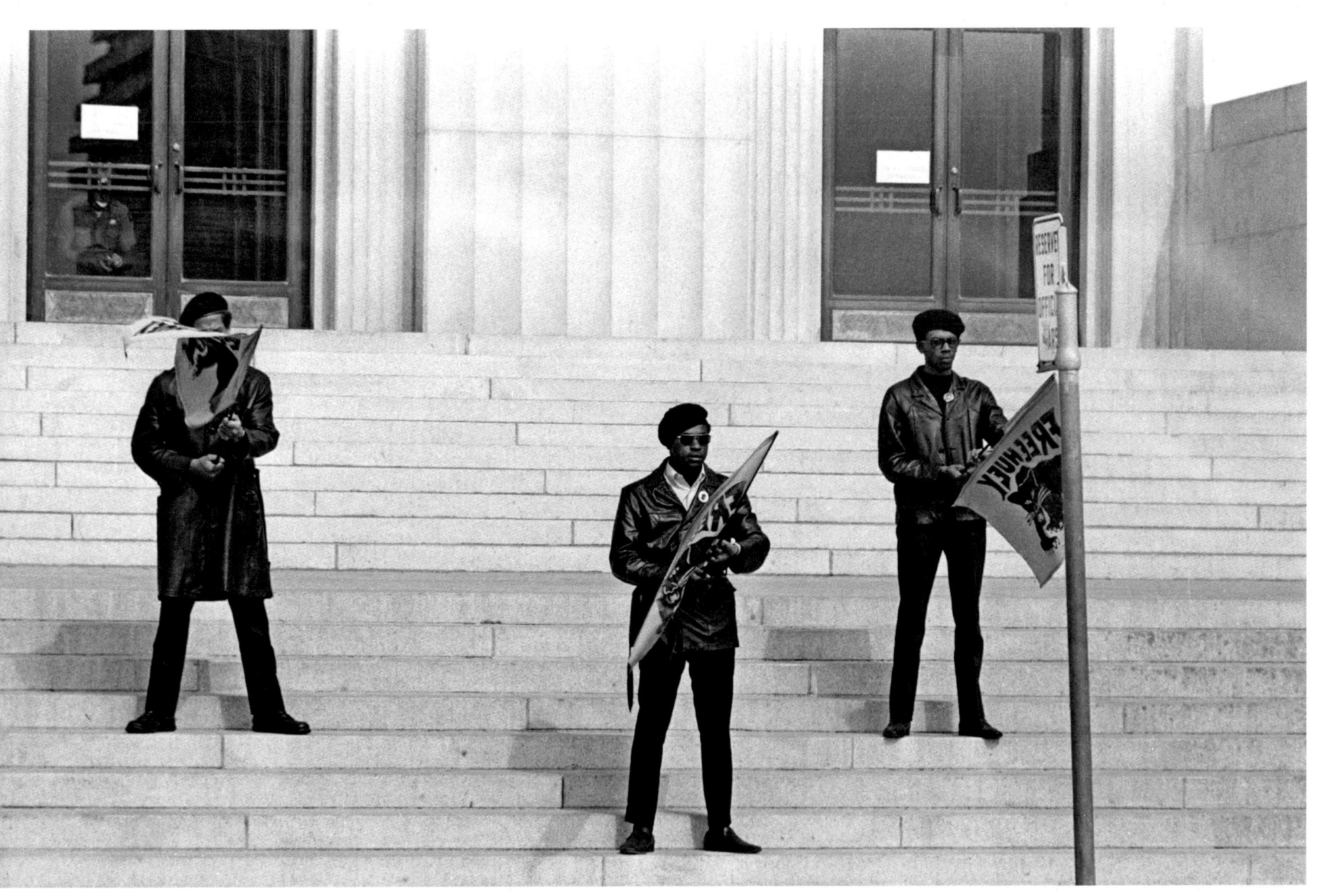
RESERVED
FOR
OFFICIAL
CARS
FREE HUEY

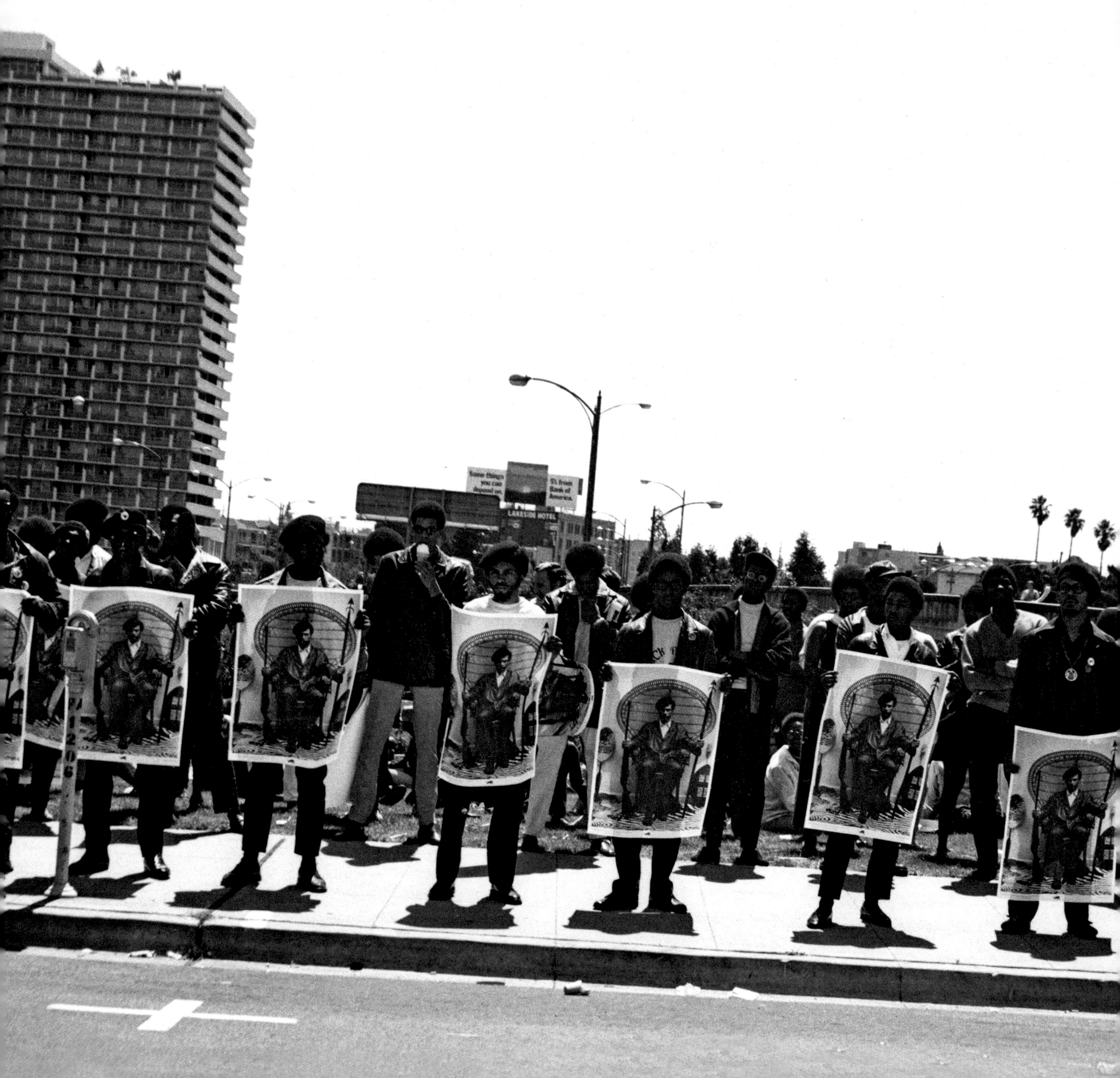

Some things
you can
depend on.
5% from
Bank of
America.
LAKESIDE HOTEL

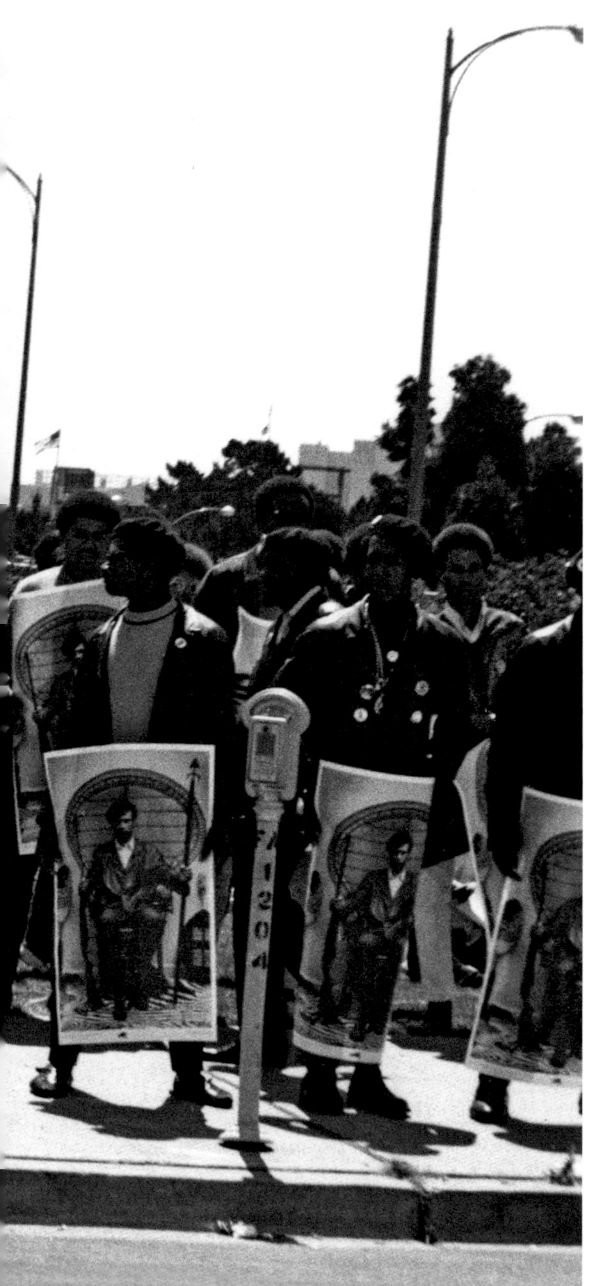

Panthers outside the Alameda County Courthouse, Oakland, California, in 1968 holding the famous portrait poster of Huey Newton. In the 1990s my father, Emmet, revealed to me that he had assisted his friend, the photographer Blair Stapp, in making that iconic Panther image at the home of Beverly Axelrod, who was a family friend and Eldridge Cleaver's attorney.

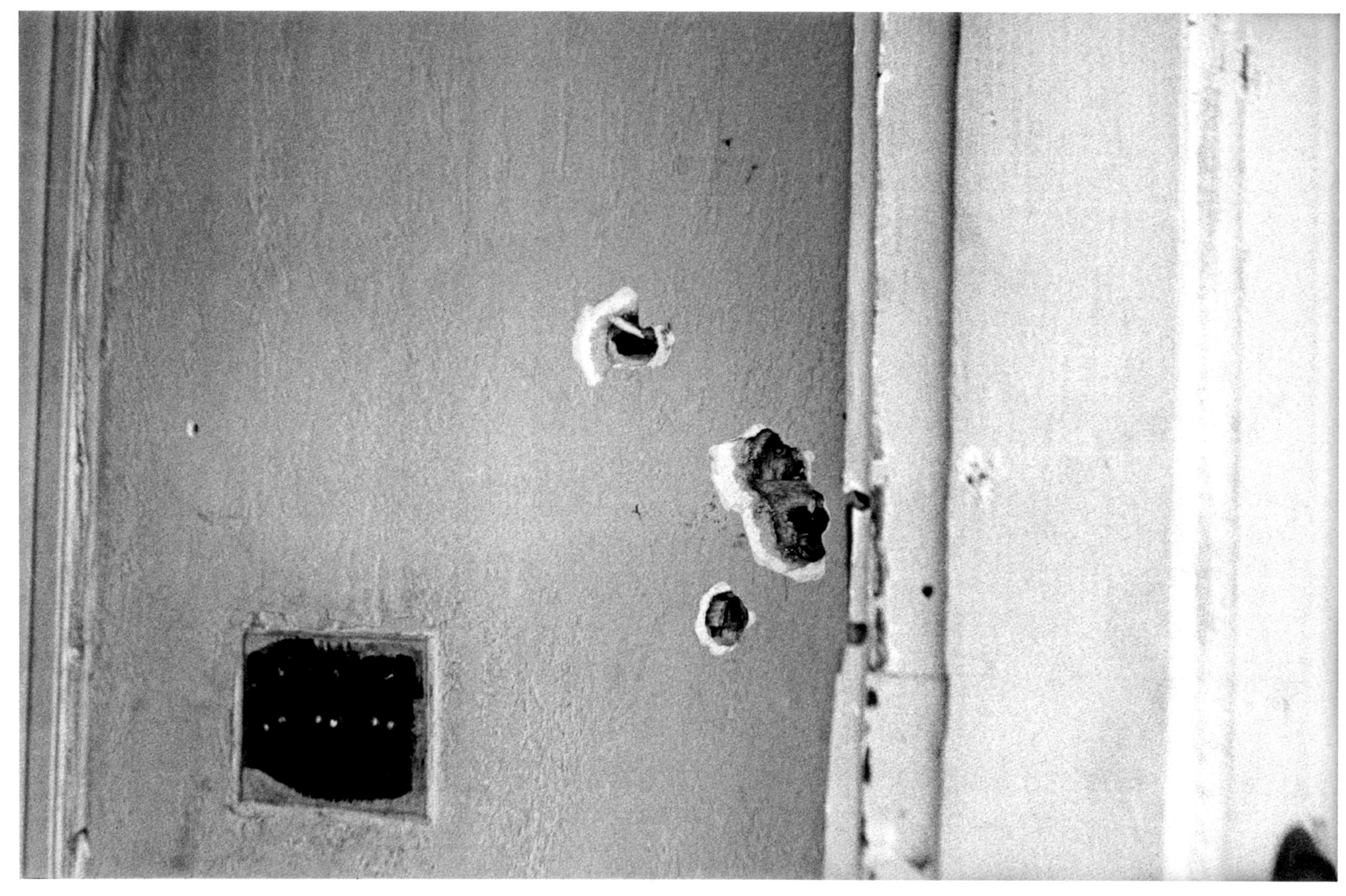

On Thursday, April 4, 1968, Dr. Martin Luther King Jr. was assassinated in Memphis. The following Saturday, in Oakland, 17-year-old Bobby Hutton, a member of the Black Panthers, was killed by the Oakland police. Lil' Bobby, just a few years older than me, died in a hail of police bullets as he surrendered with his hands raised, clad only in his underwear. He had emerged, along with Eldridge Cleaver, from the basement of this house in West Oakland that had been firebombed by the police.

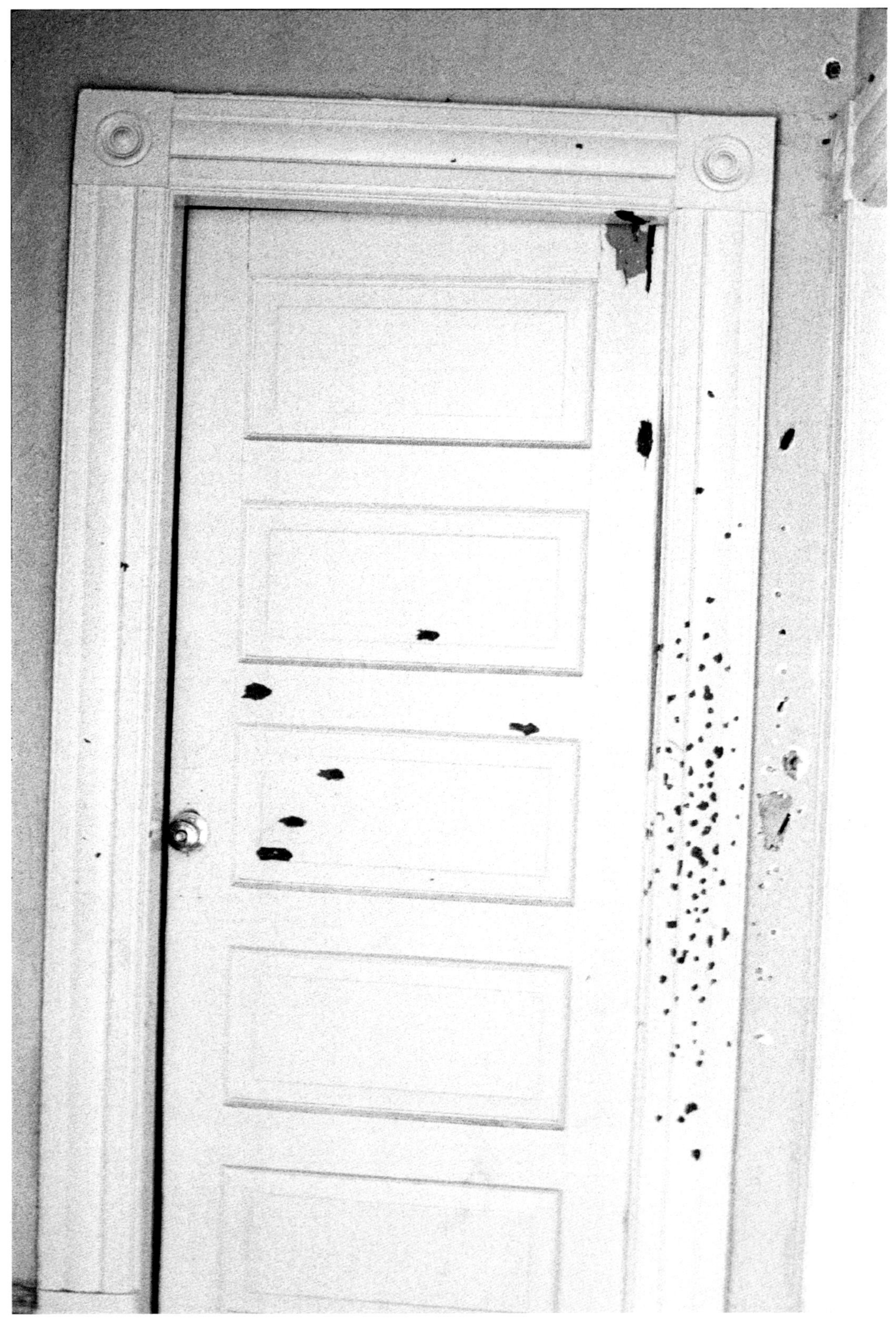

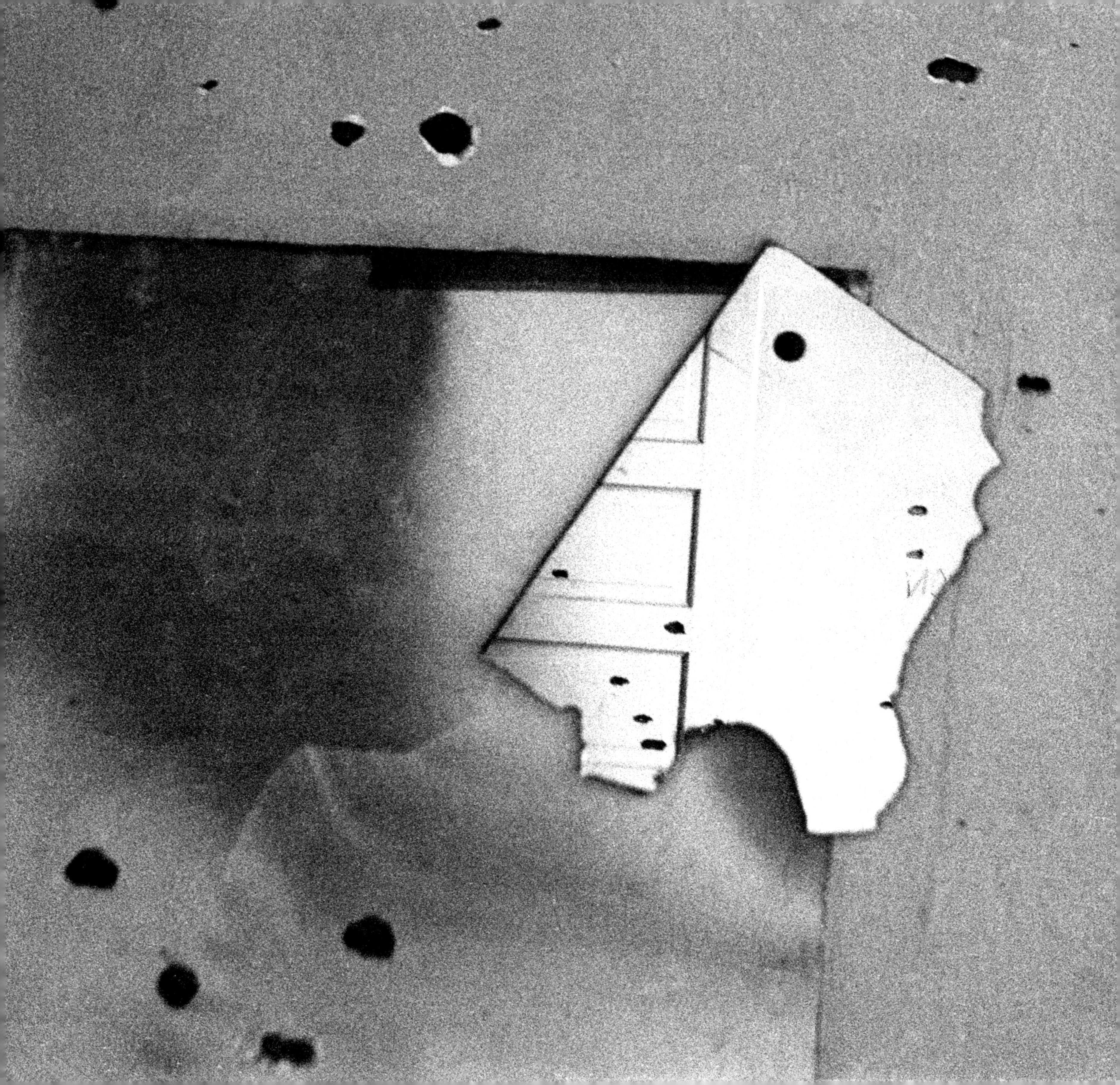

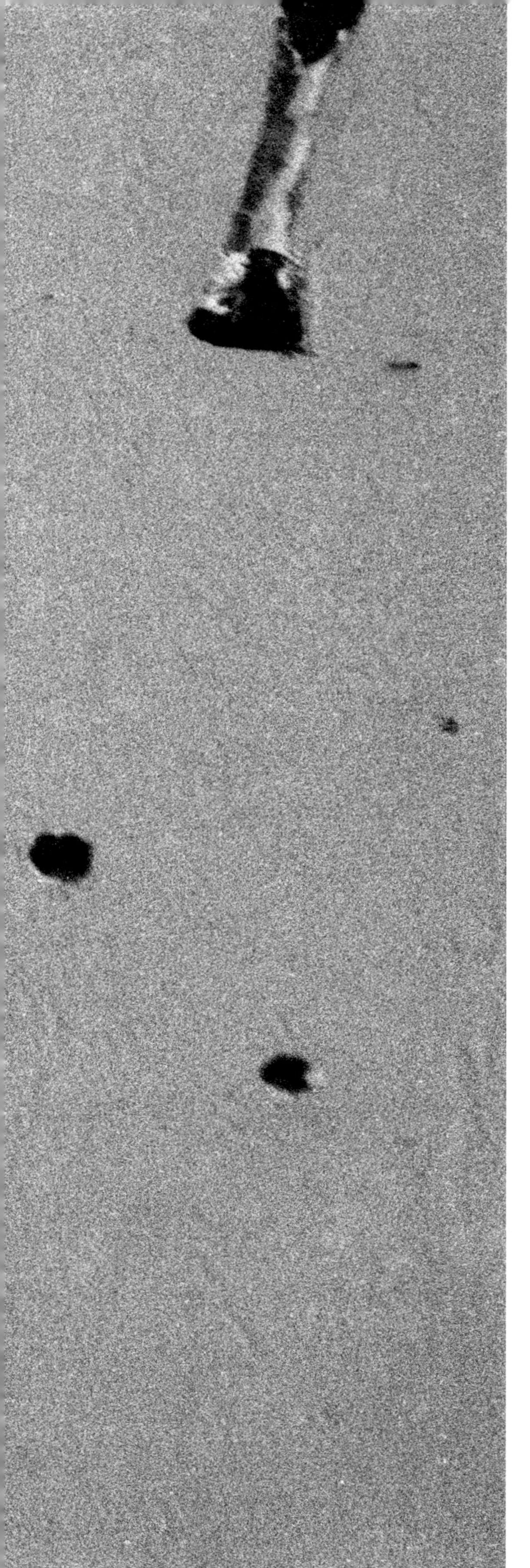

The smell of burnt wood and the acrid stench of tear gas and gunfire filled the rooms like a horrifyingly pungent incense. It was like an eerie open-house tour, except the walls were riddled with hundreds of bullet holes, shattered glass filled the floors, and the suffocating ghosts of the previous night's deaths stole the air from each room.

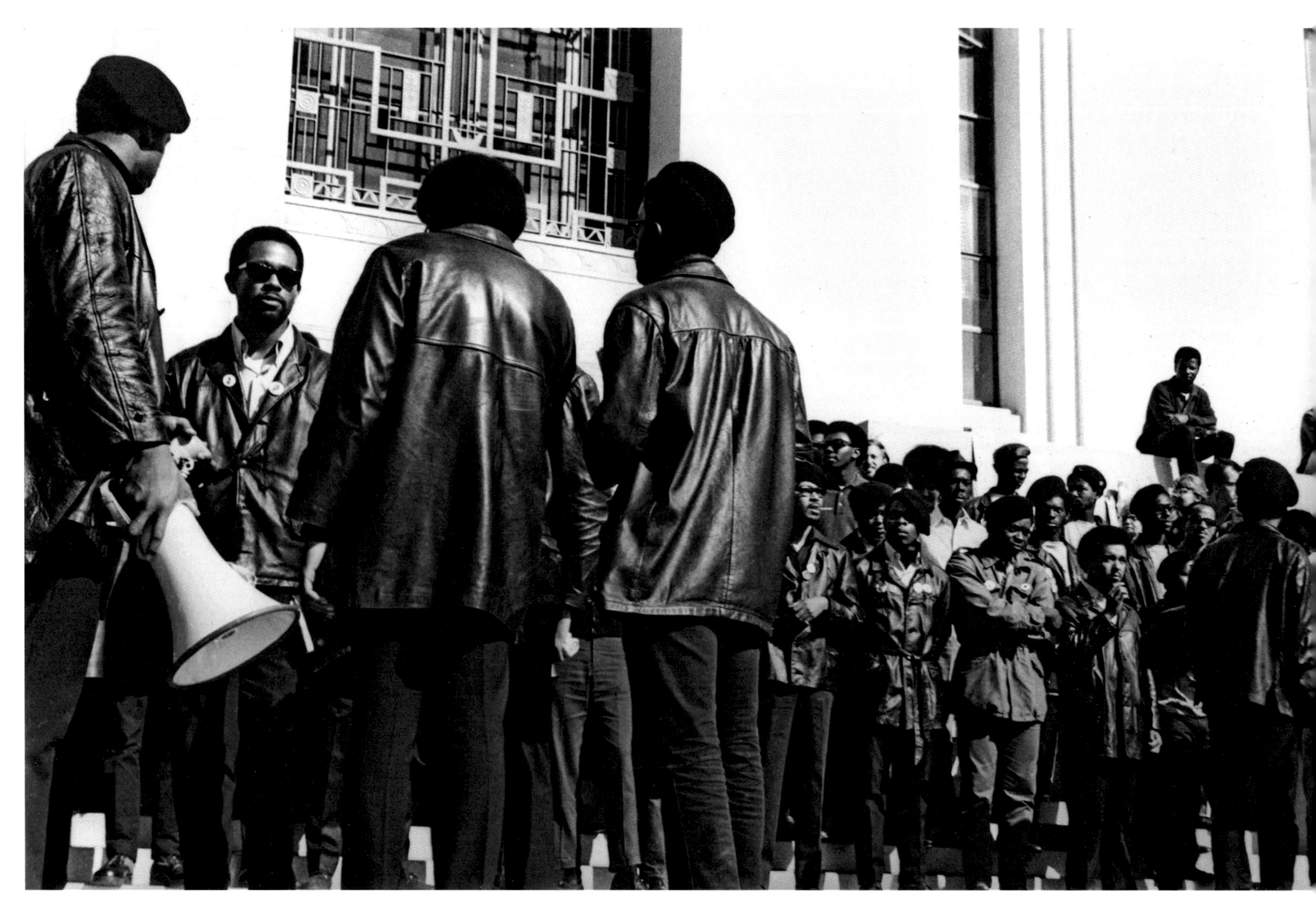

Eldridge Cleaver and Panthers on the steps of the Alameda County Courthouse during the Huey Newton trial. Opposite page, Emory Douglas, left, and other Panthers across the street

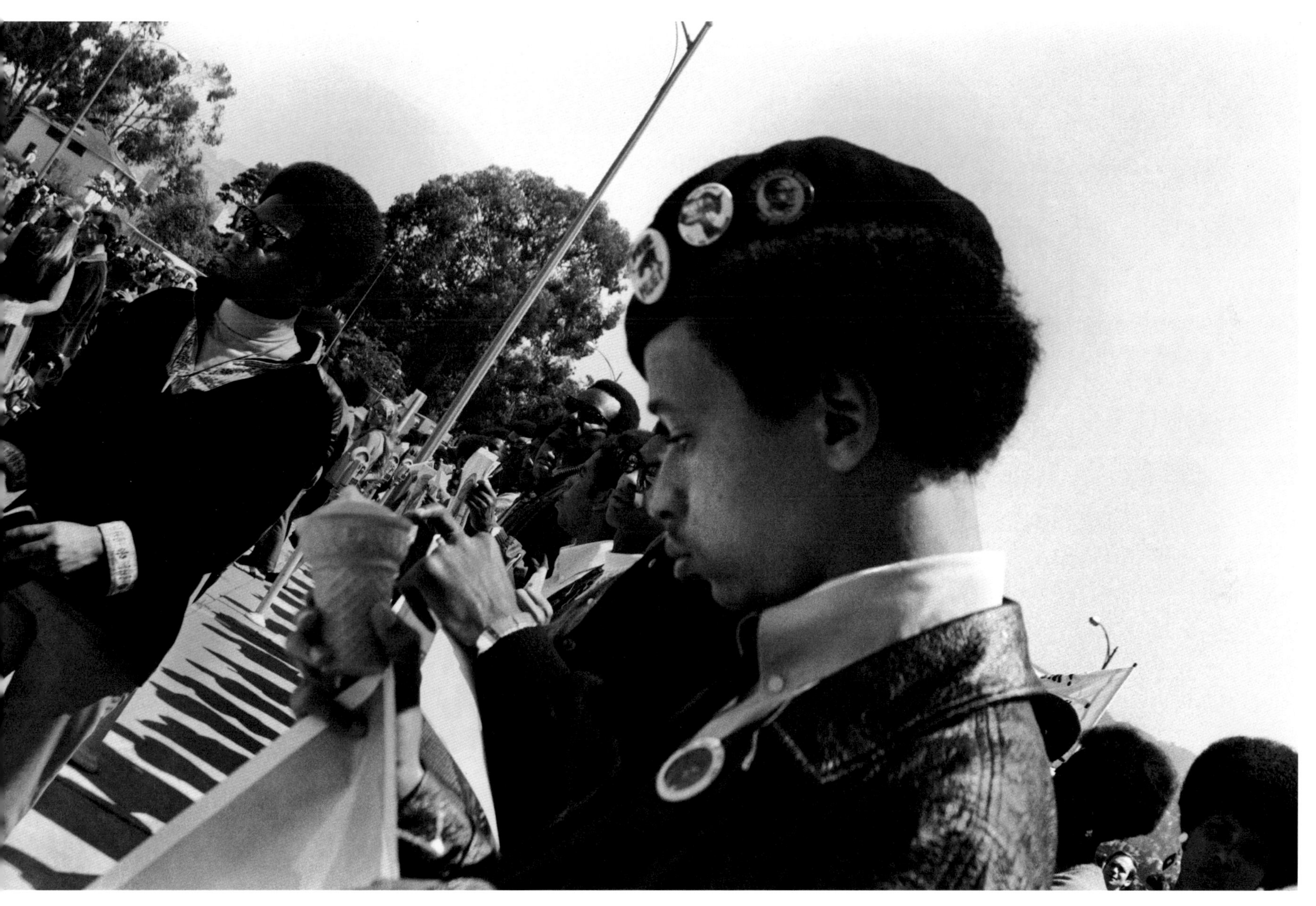

The Panthers staged a variety of well-choreographed security perimeters and public protest events around the Alameda County Courthouse. These events highlighted the excitement of the Black Panther movement that was crystallized in their visuals: Blackness, black berets and black leather!

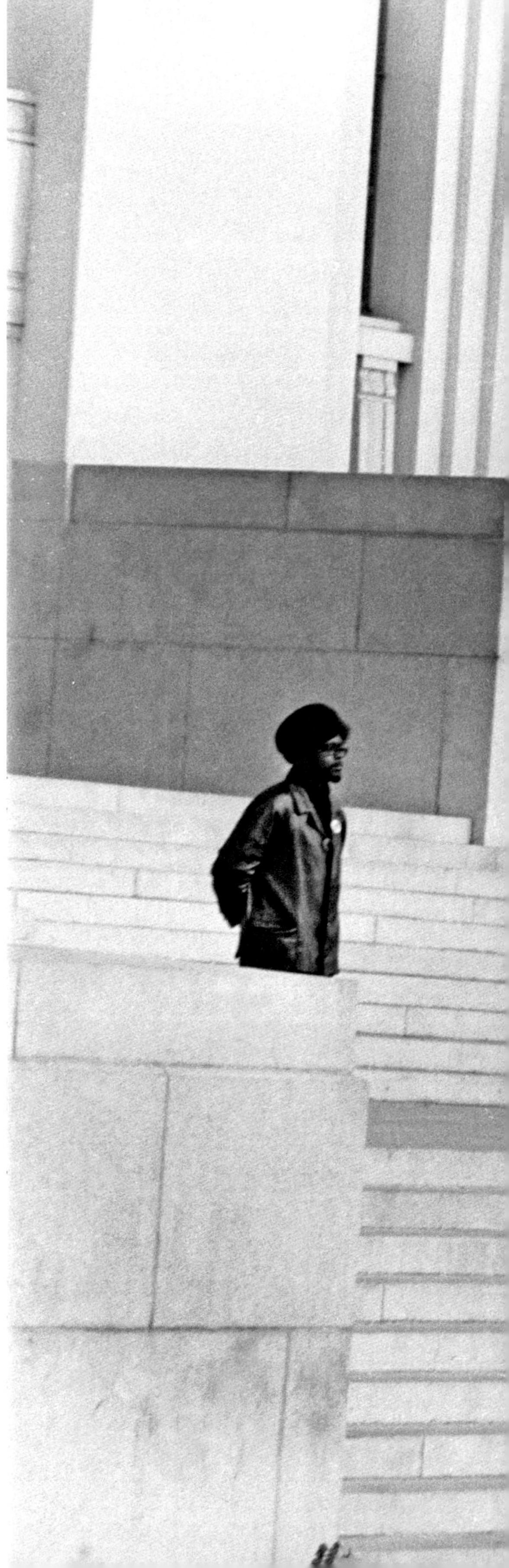

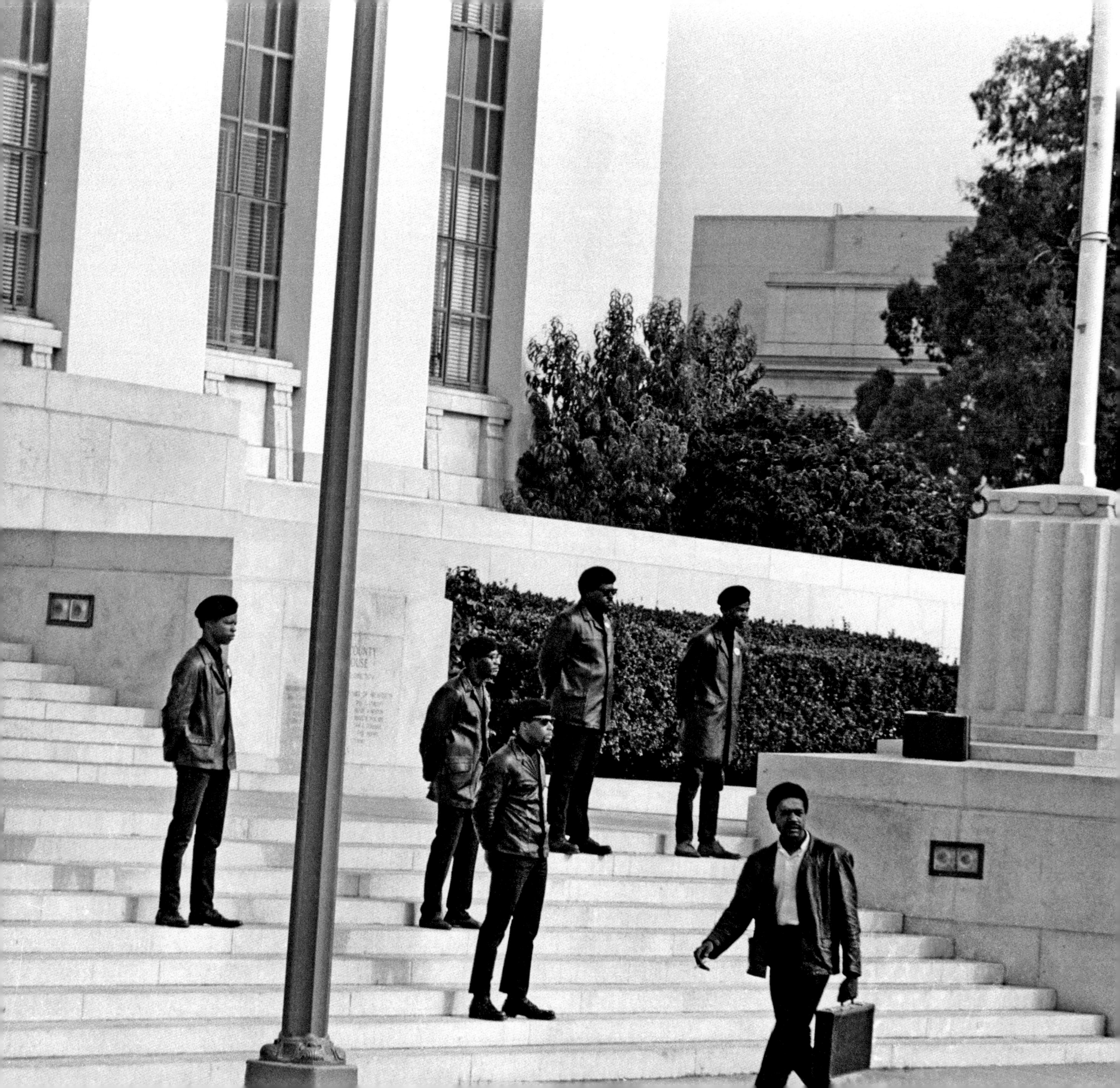

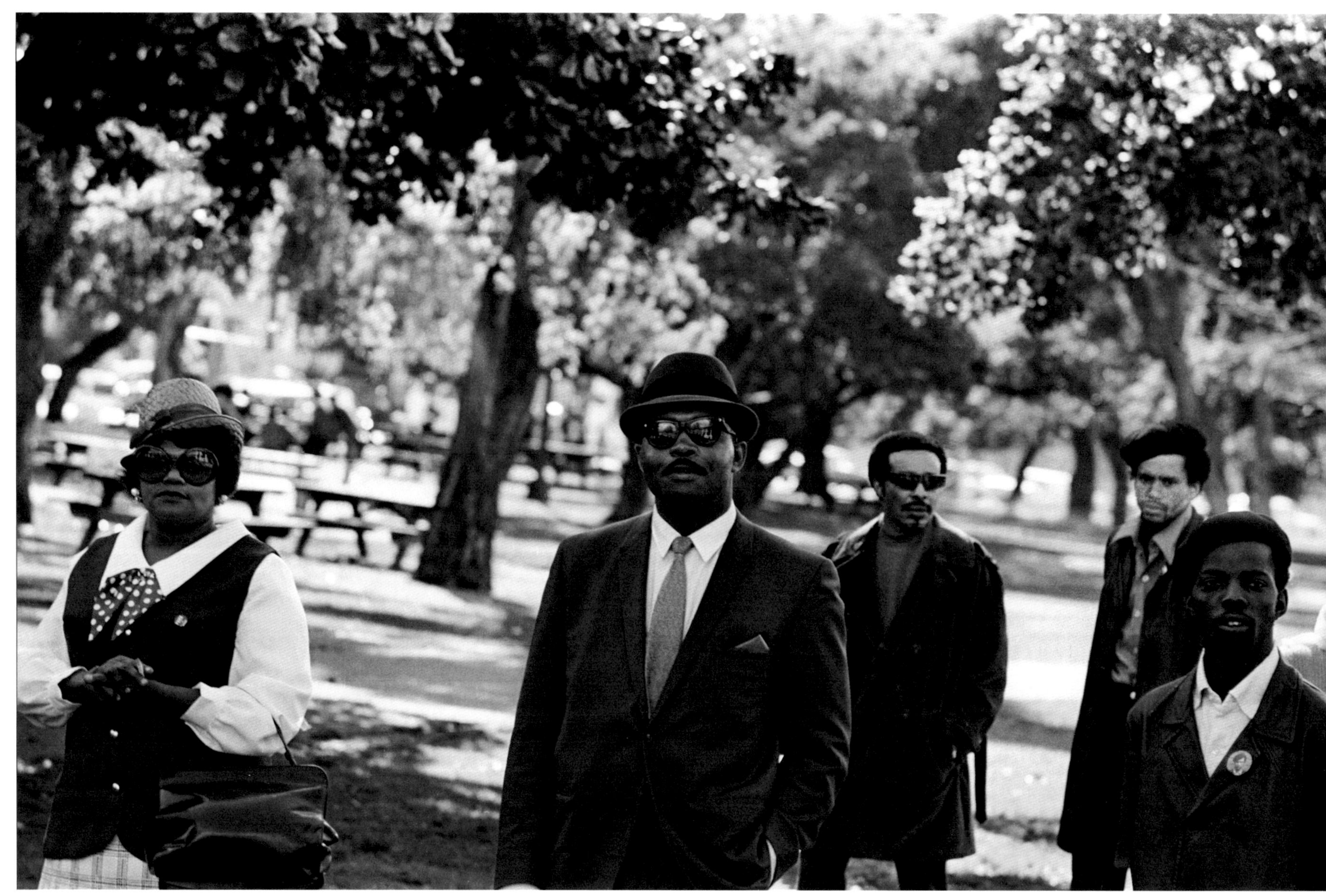

In 1968 the Panthers began to have frequent rallies and events, including education classes for Panther members and community food programs at Oakland's DeFremery Park. The grounds around the Victorian mansion built for the wealthy de Fremery family had been converted into Oakland's first municipal playground in 1907; in the following decades it was a frequent location for progressive political programs and events. In 1968 it was unofficially renamed Lil' Bobby Hutton Park, after the first official member of the Panthers and the first member to be killed by police. In 2016 the City Council officially renamed a grove of trees in the park in his honor.

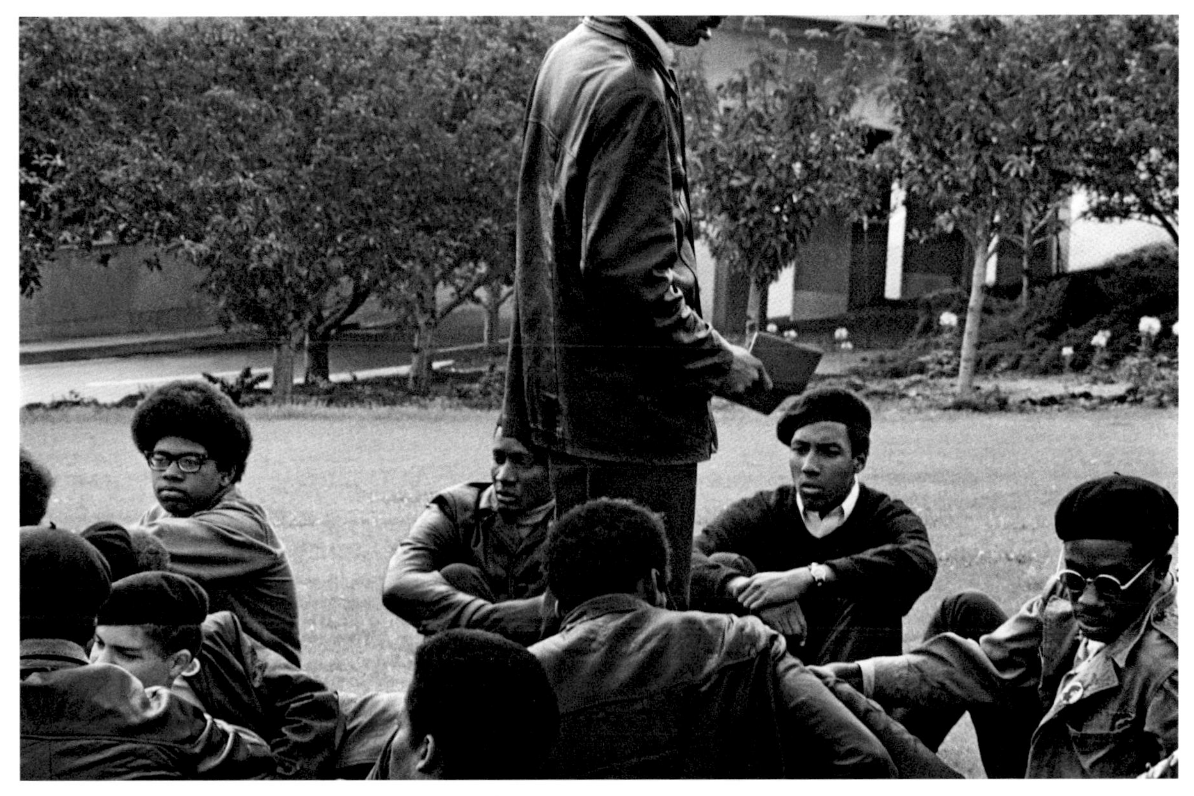

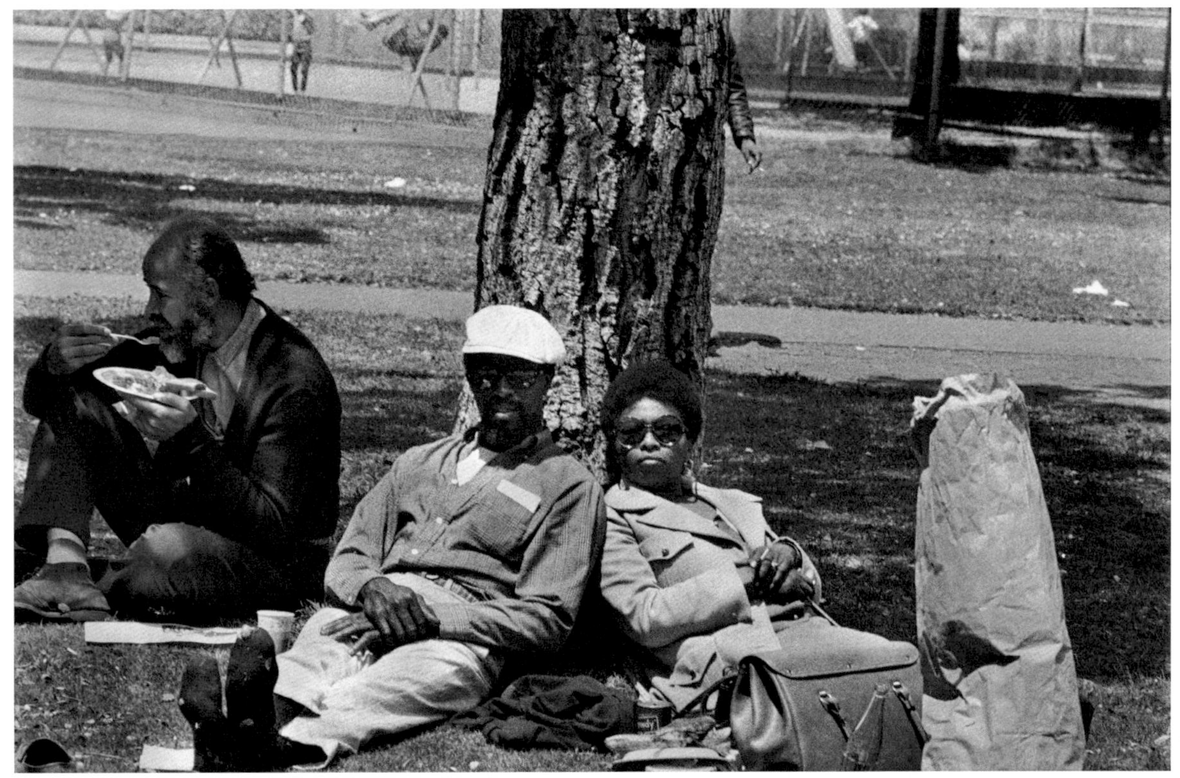

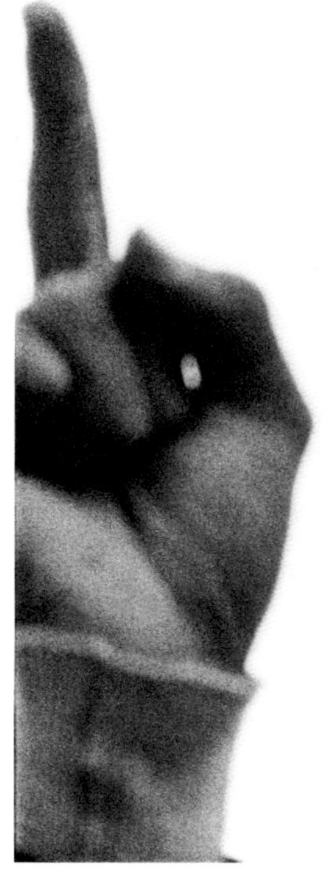

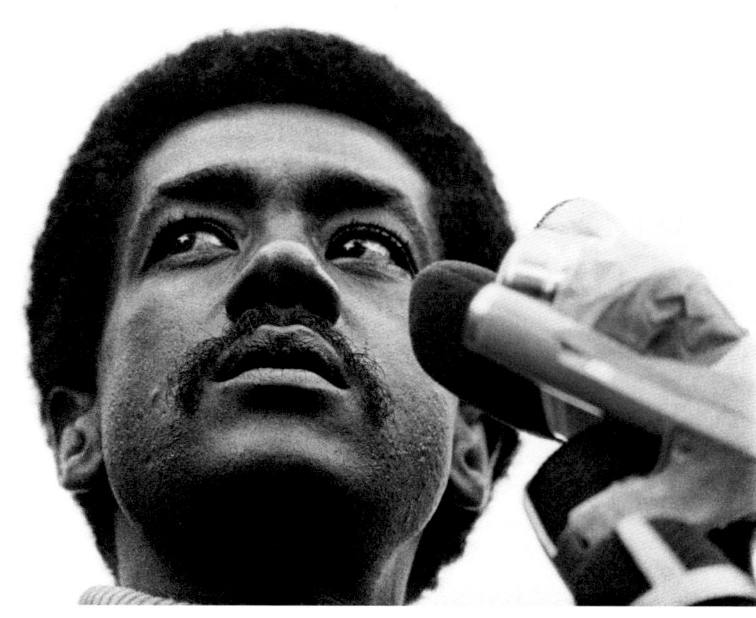

Bobby Seale at a rally at DeFremery Park, August 25, 1968.

Marsha Taylor speaking at a May Day rally in San Francisco in 1969.

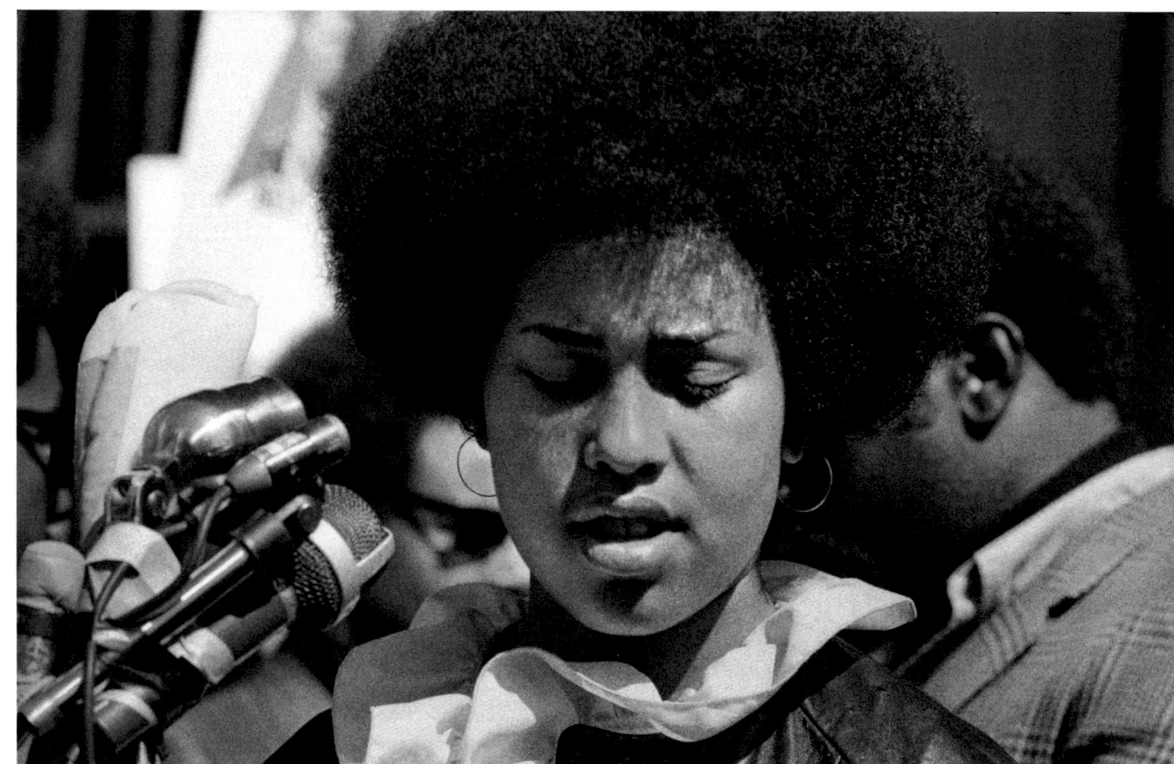

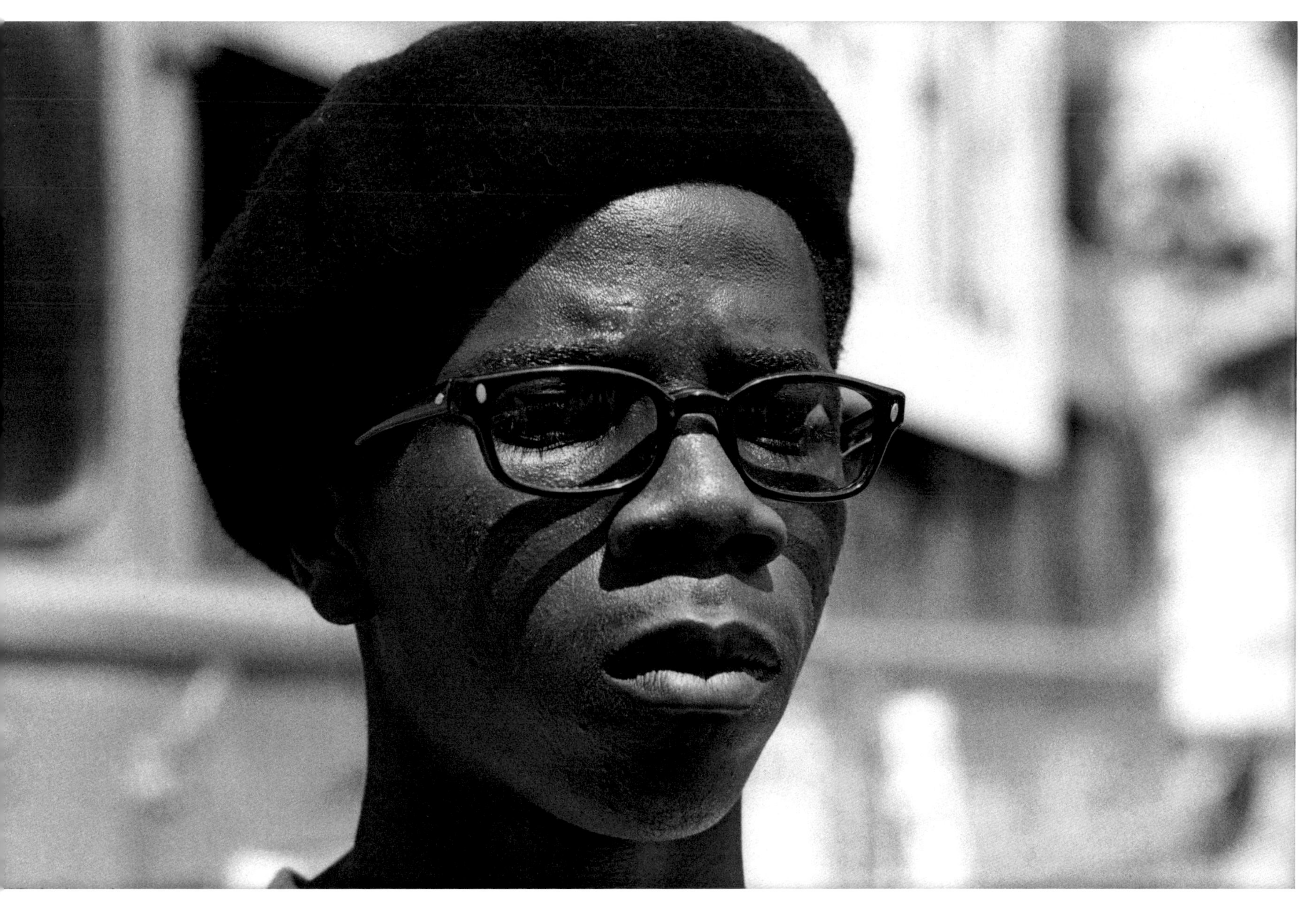

Panther member on security at DeFremery Park, July 14, 1968.

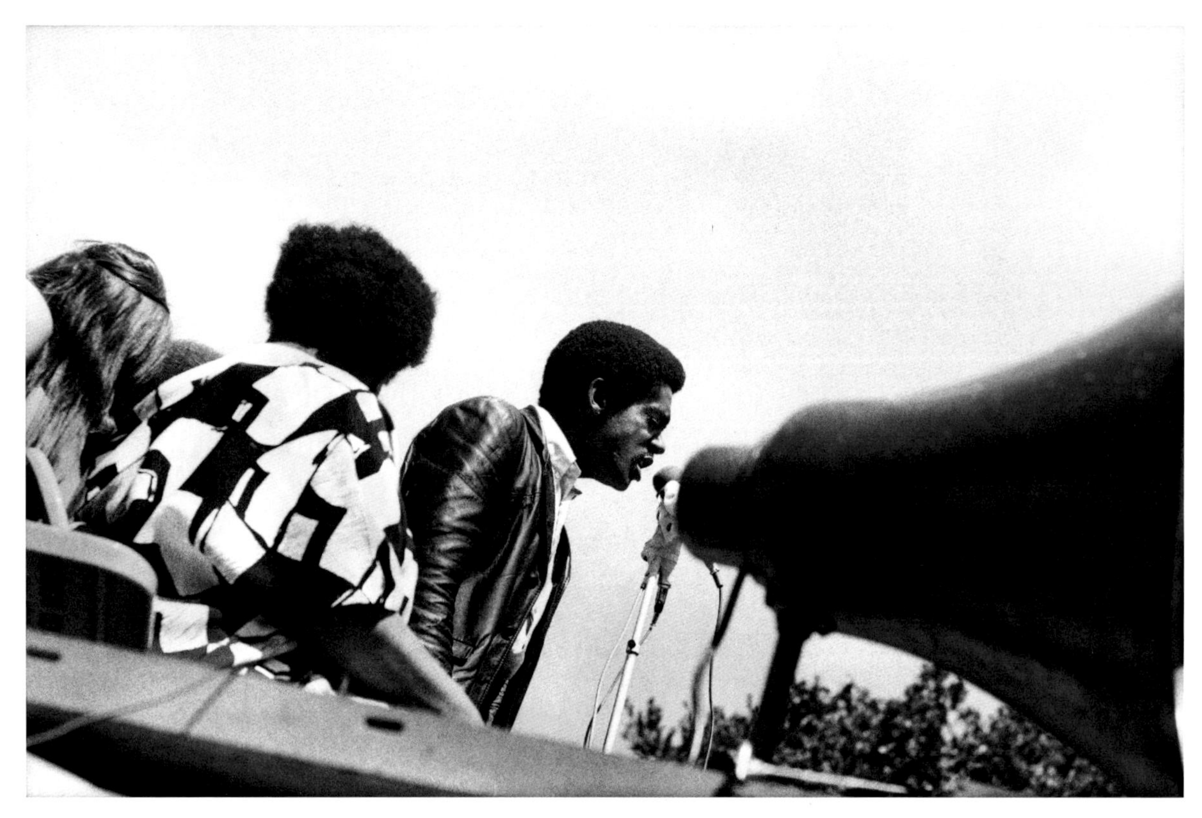

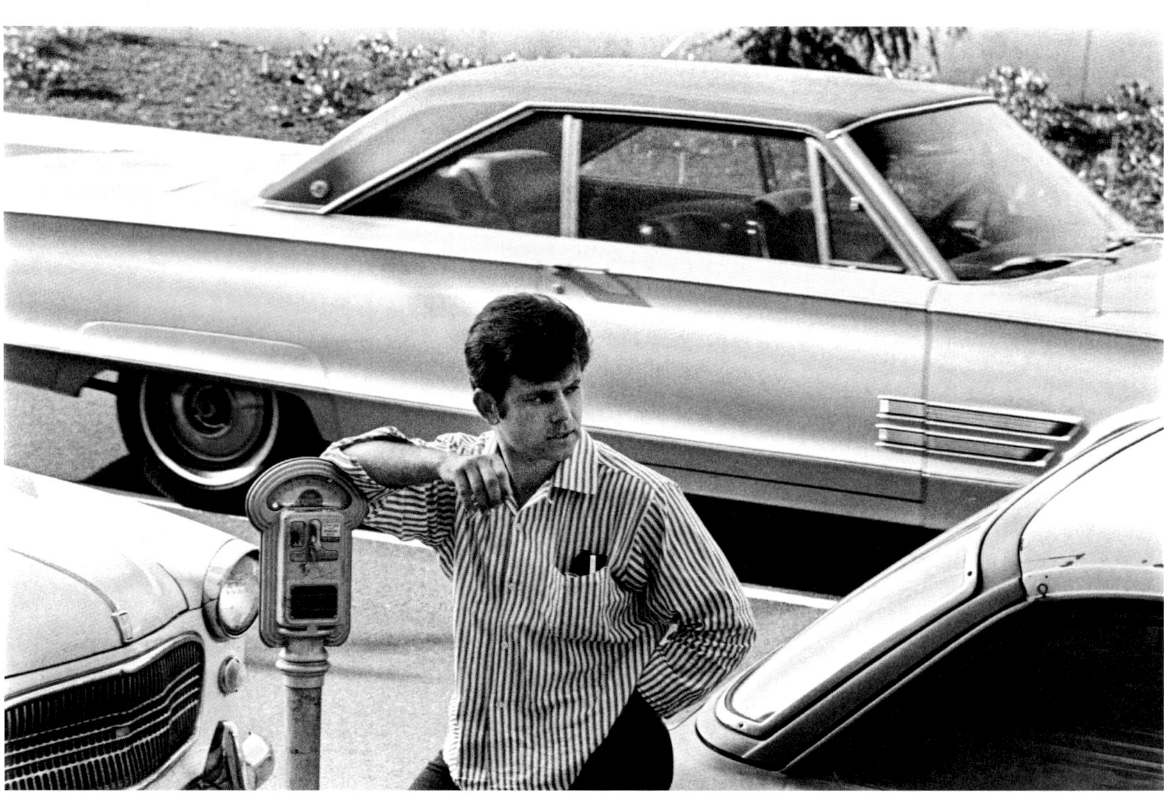

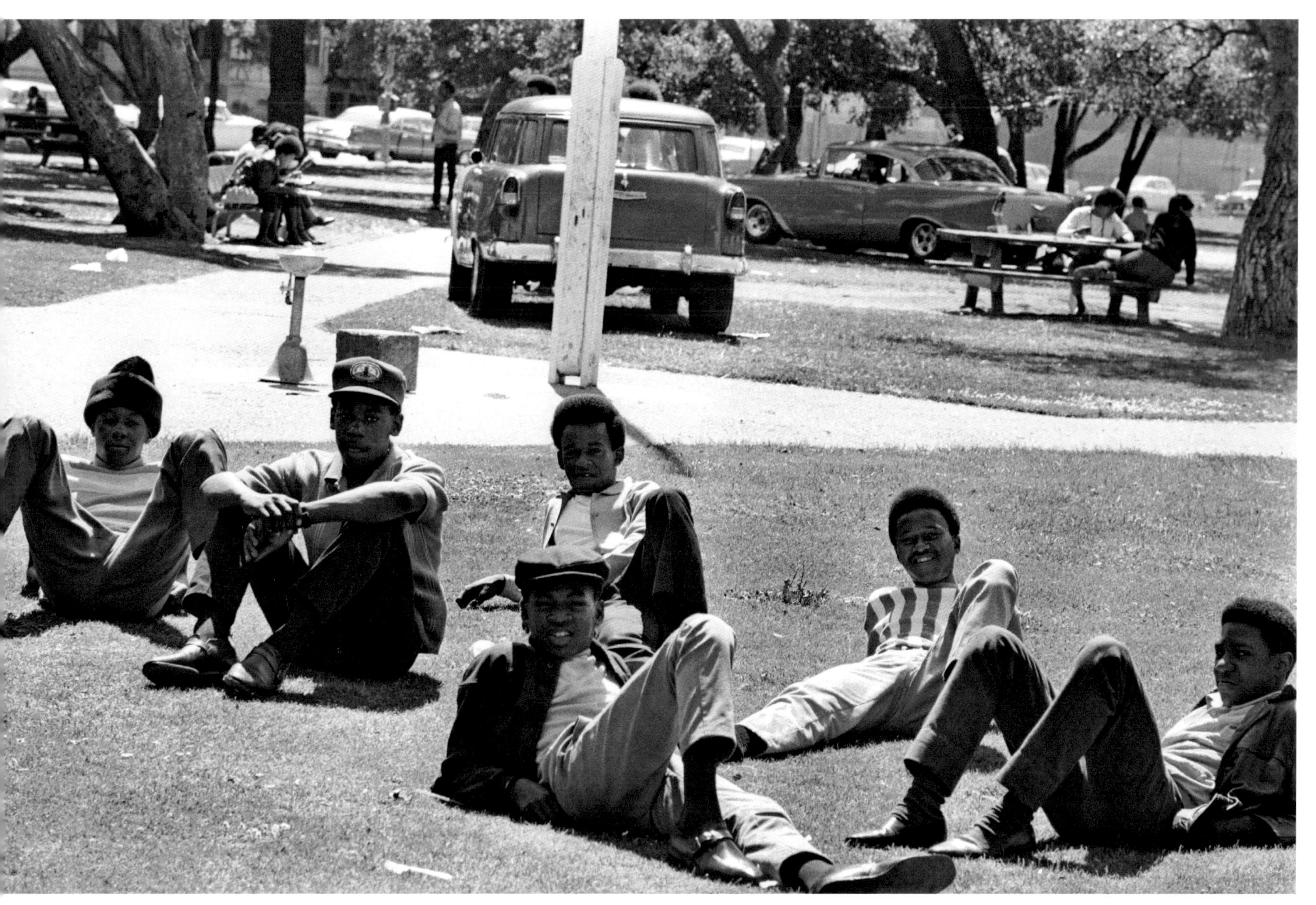

DeFremery Park, 1968. Above, community youth; opposite page top,
Bobby Seale; bottom, unidentified man on the sidelines of the park.

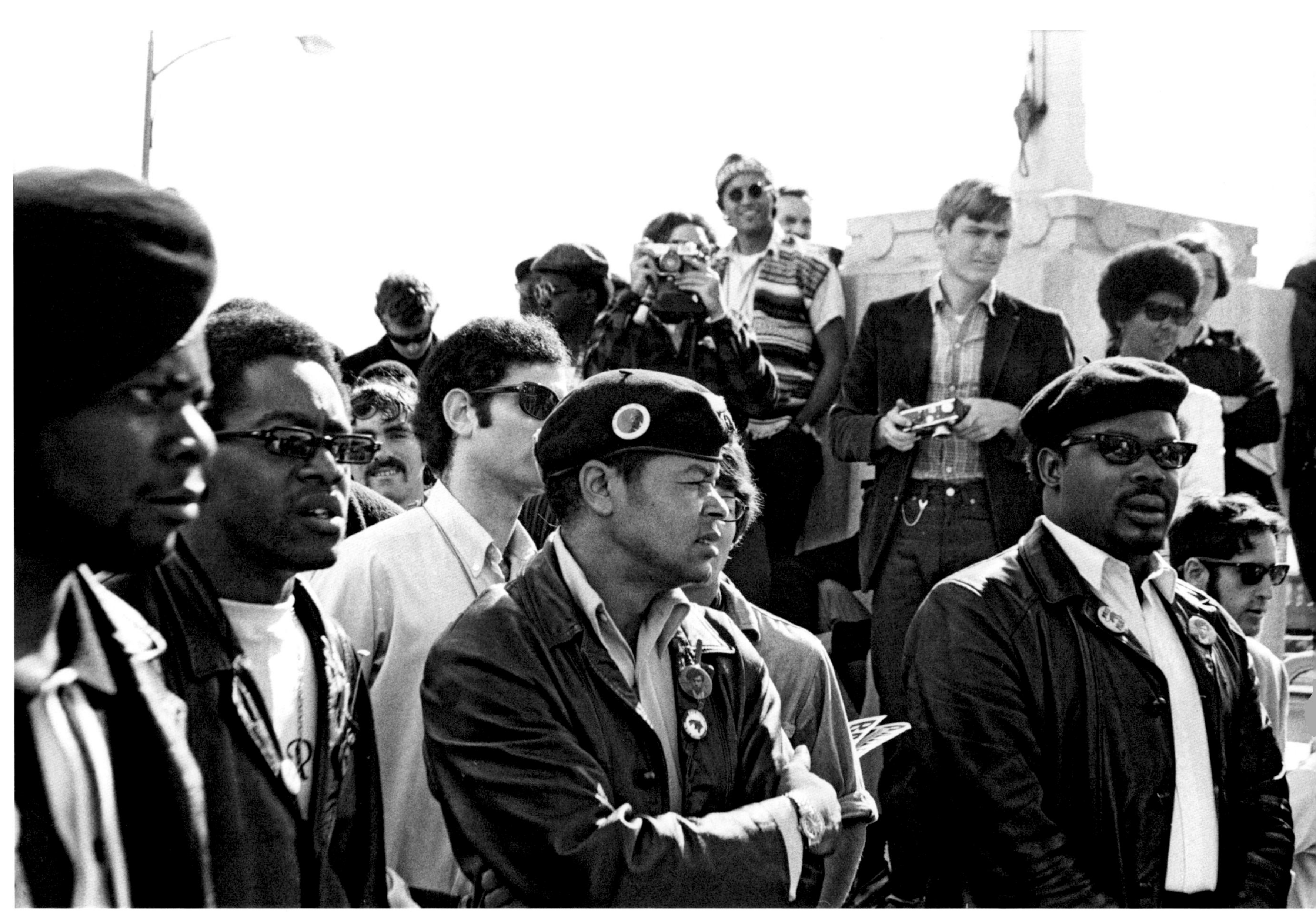
Panthers and supporters outside the Alameda County Courthouse, 1968.

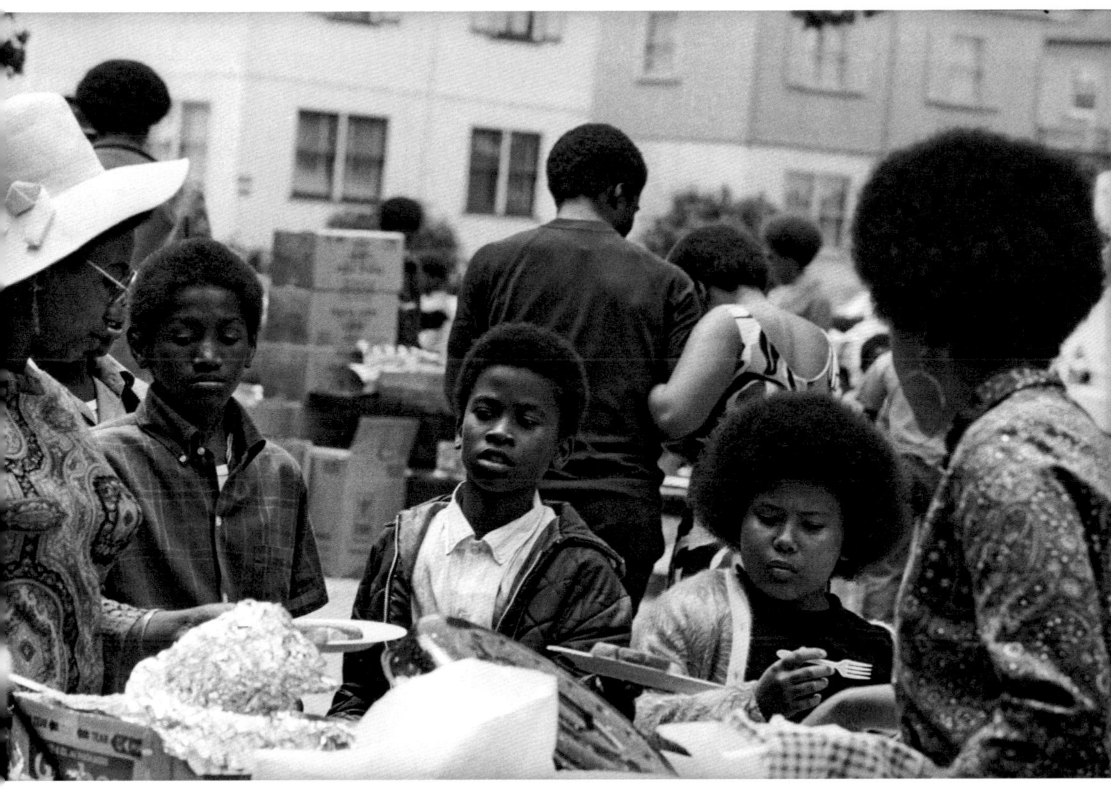

A food giveaway in Campbell Village in West Oakland, 1968.

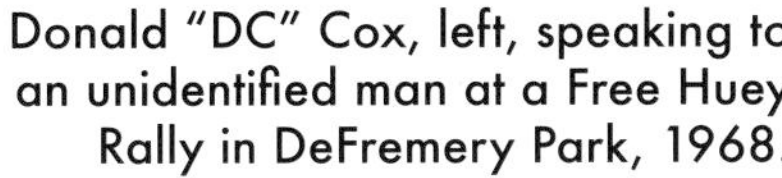

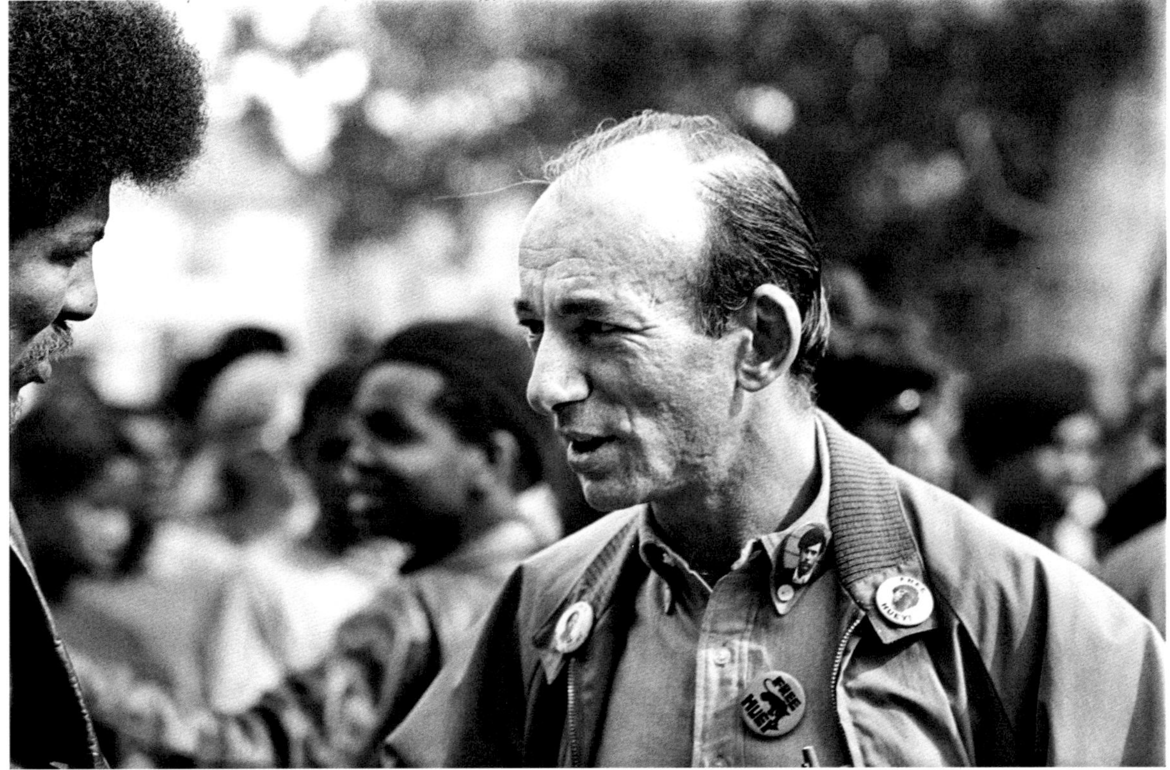

Donald "DC" Cox, left, speaking to an unidentified man at a Free Huey Rally in DeFremery Park, 1968.

Members of the Los Angeles chapter of the Black Panthers on guard duty during a rally at DeFremery Park in 1968. Second from right is John Huggins, the chapter's leader. He was killed, along with Bunchy Carter, a fellow Panther, at the University of California, Los Angeles, campus in January 1969. They were shot during an altercation with members of US, a black nationalist organization, that reportedly was incited by undercover government agents.

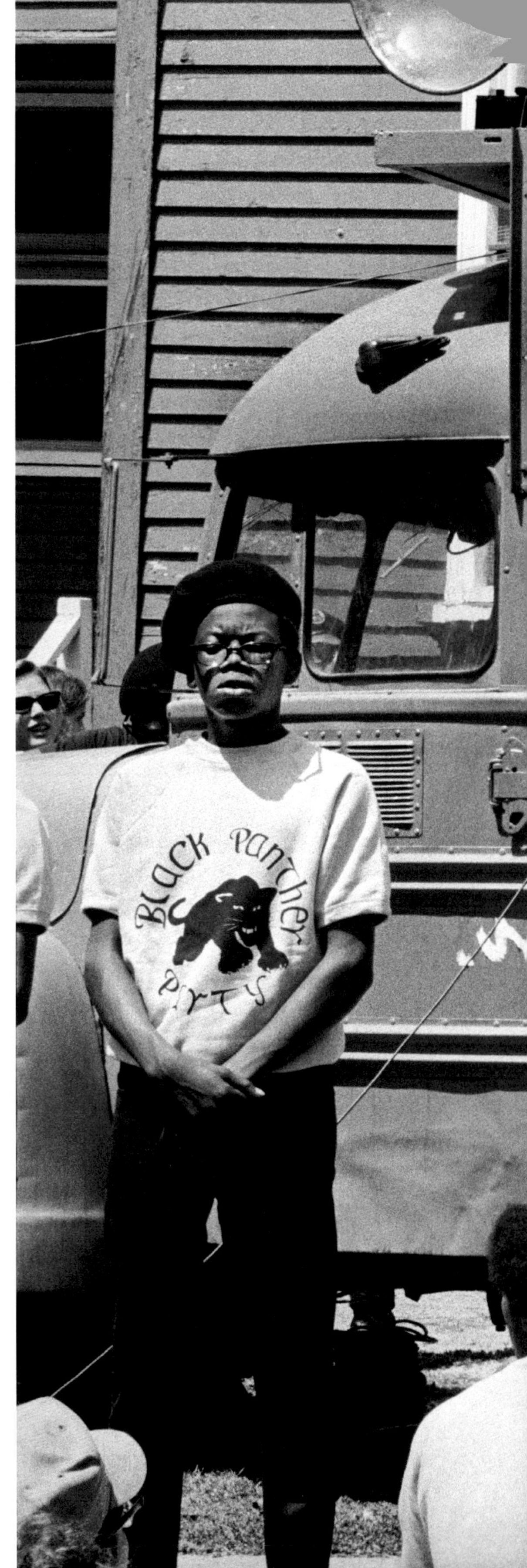

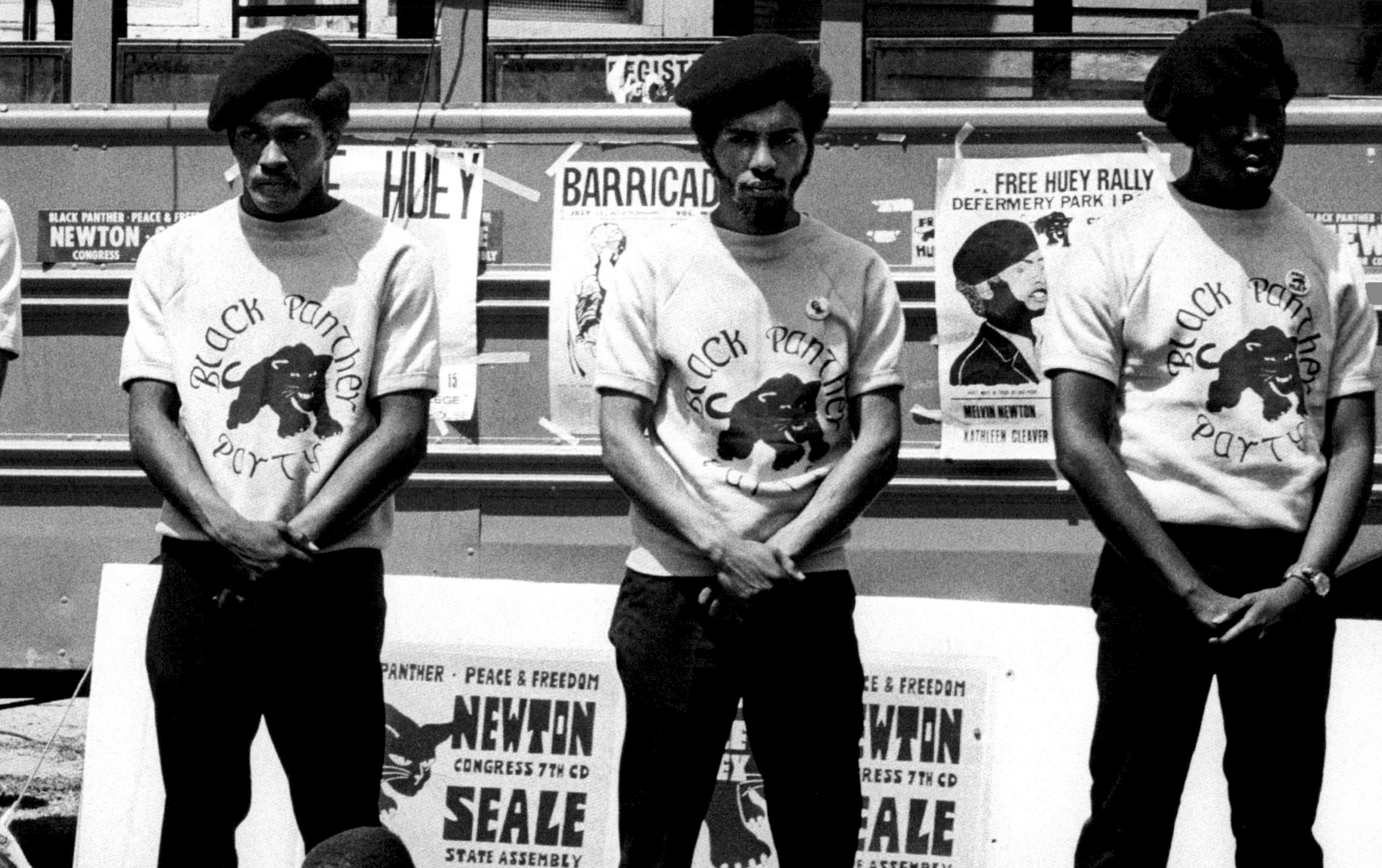

FREE HUEY
BLACK PANTHER PARTY
HUEY
BARRICADE
FREE HUEY RALLY
DEFERMERY PARK
MELVIN NEWTON
KATHLEEN CLEAVER
BLACK PANTHER · PEACE & FREEDOM
NEWTON
CONGRESS
PANTHER · PEACE & FREEDOM
NEWTON
CONGRESS 7TH CD
SEALE
STATE ASSEMBLY
CE & FREEDOM
EWTON
RESS 7TH CD
EALE
E ASSEMBLY

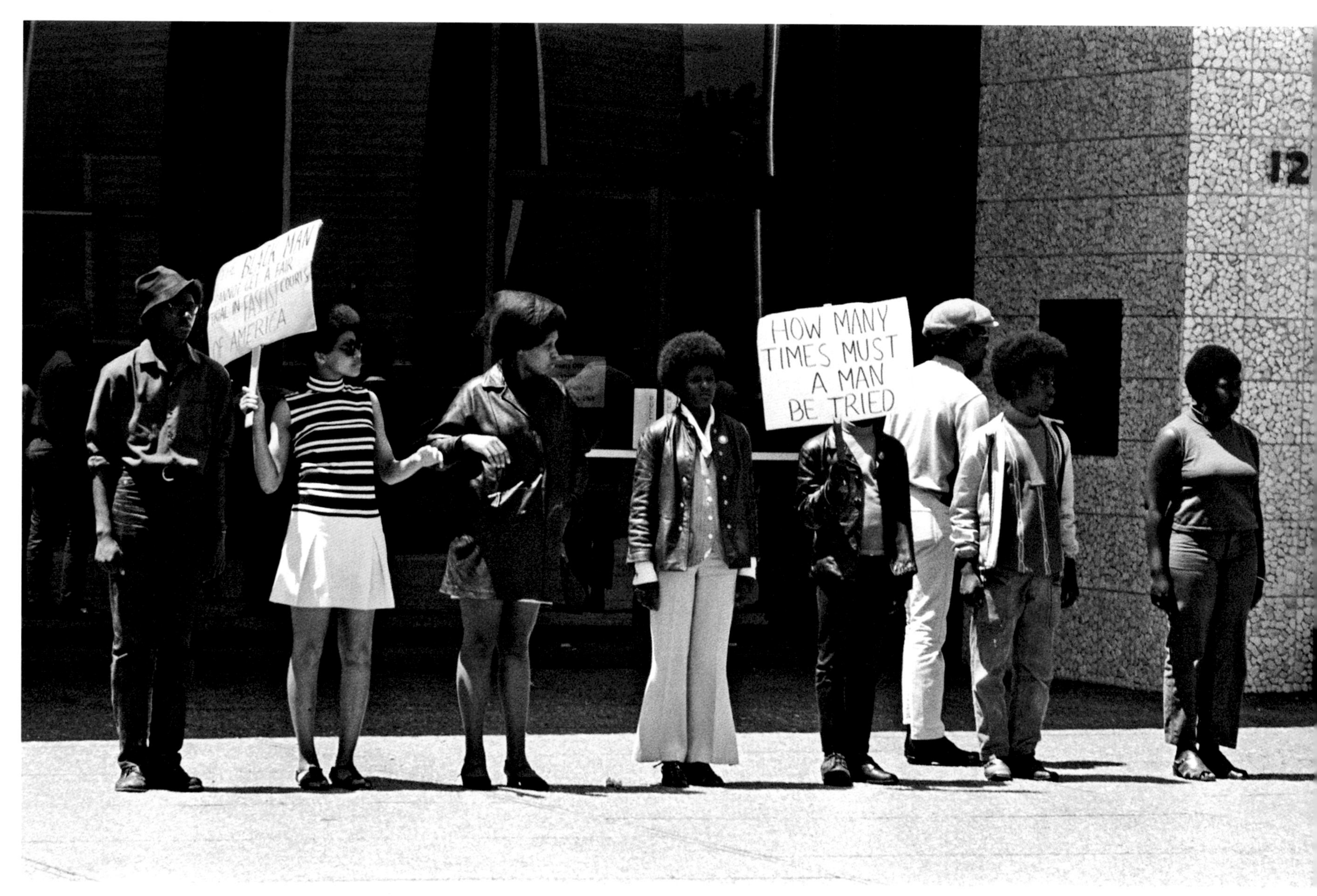


Panthers during a Free Huey rally outside the San Francisco
Federal Courthouse on May Day, 1969.

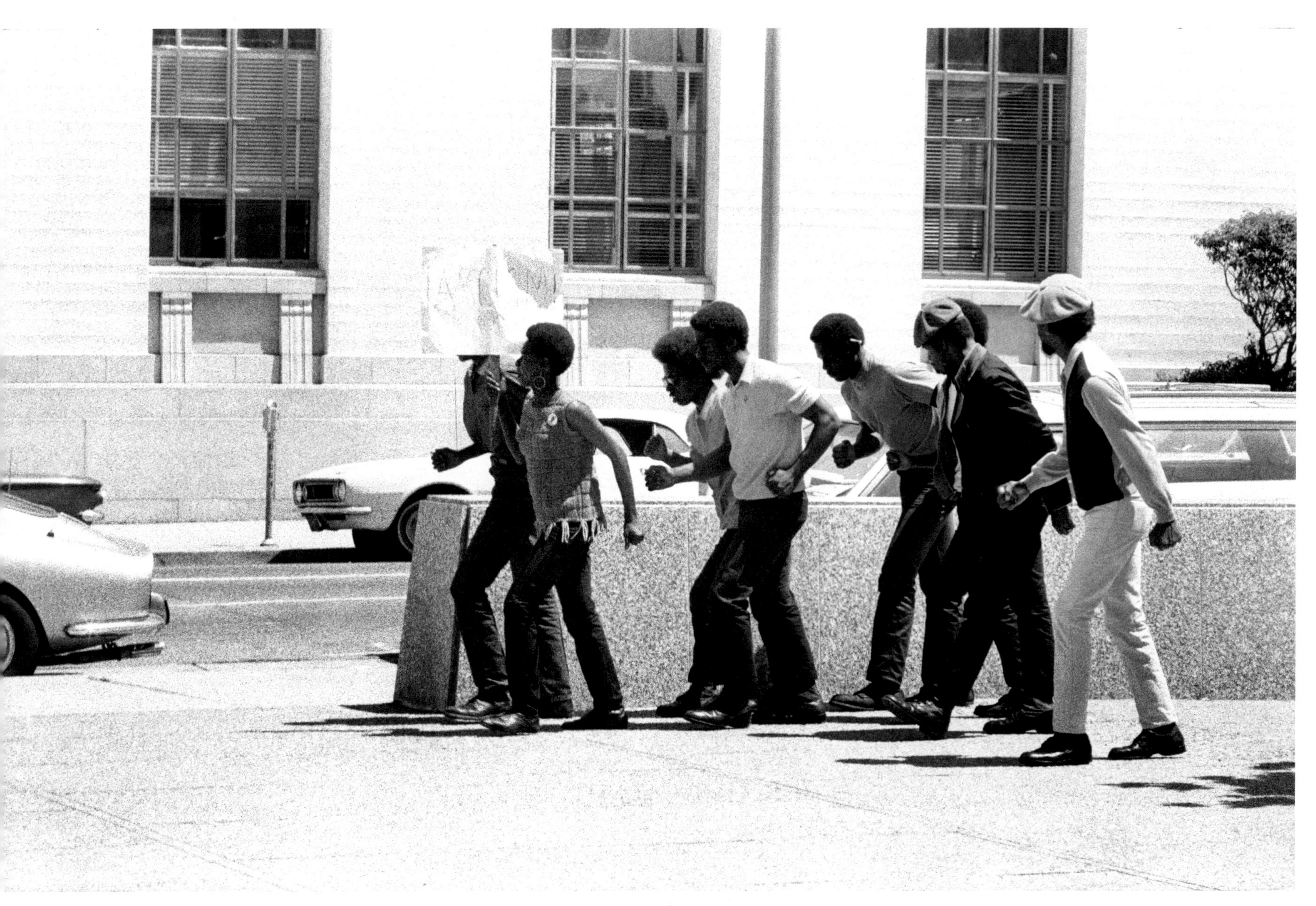

Panthers in 1969 marching outside the Alameda County Courthouse in support of members Warren Wells and Charles Bursey, who were on trial for their part in the April 6, 1968, shootout that led to the death of Bobby Hutton.

In 1969 I also made photographs during riots in Berkeley over planned construction on the grounds of People's Park, to which the university had cut off access. The first day, May 15, the police used shotguns loaded with buckshot on the protesters and bystanders, killing one, blinding another and injuring dozens on what became known as "Bloody Thursday."

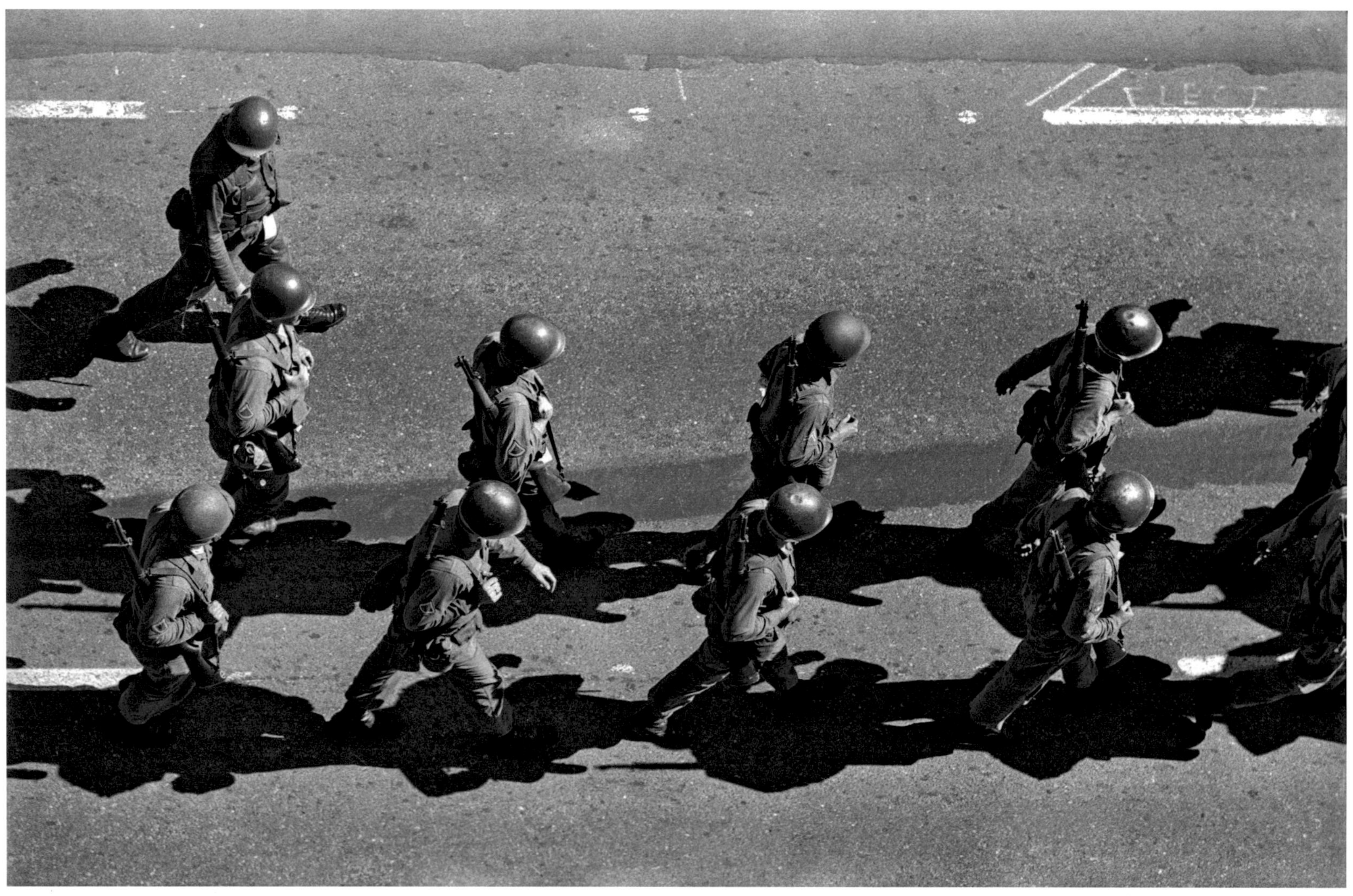

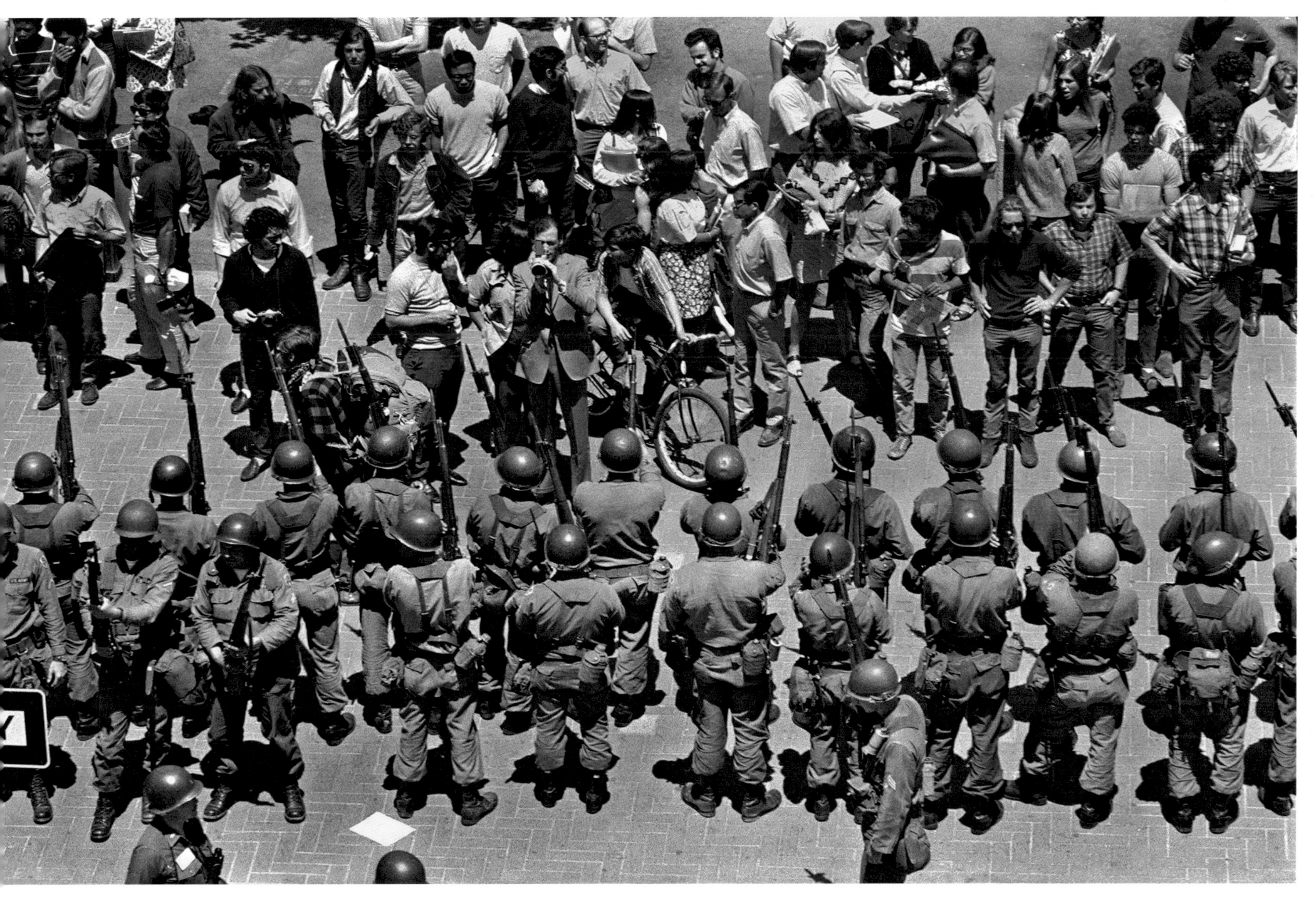

Above and opposite page, National Guard troops on the campus
of the University of California, Berkeley, May 19, 1969.

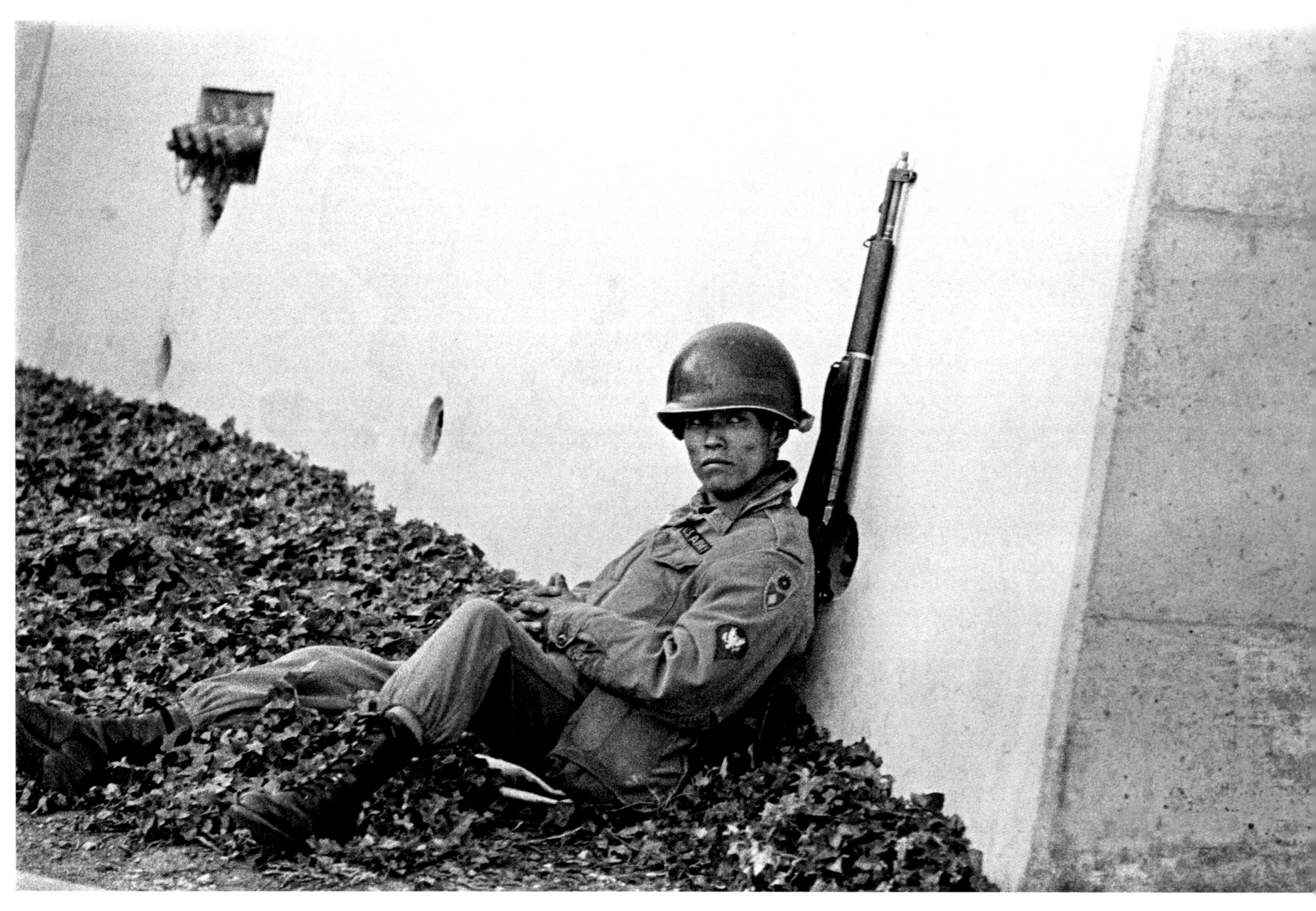

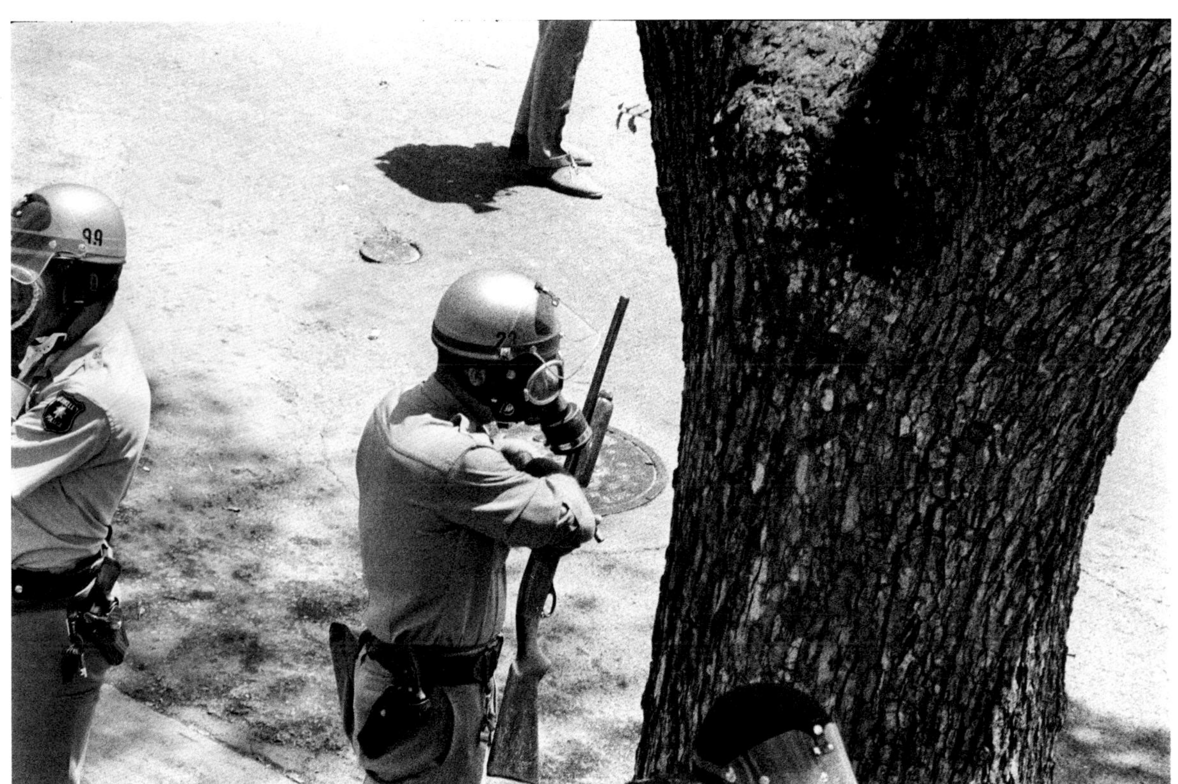

e were the only times I've been
at — twice by the police during
e riots in Berkeley.

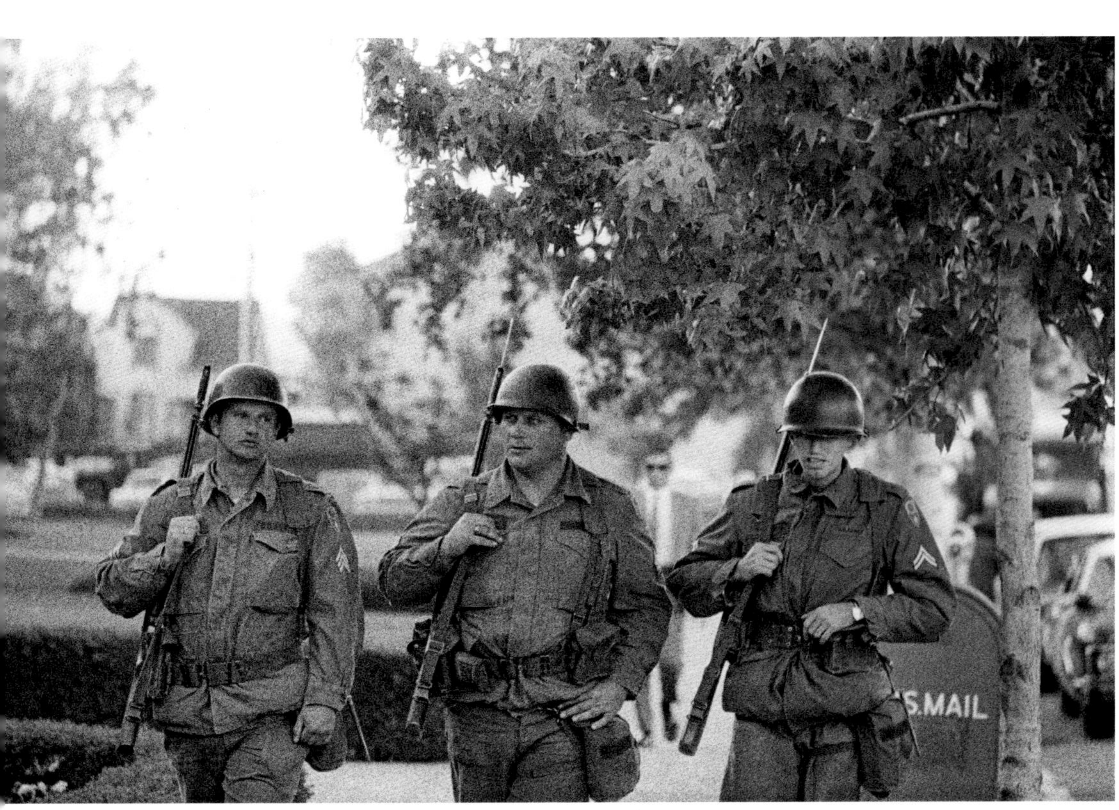

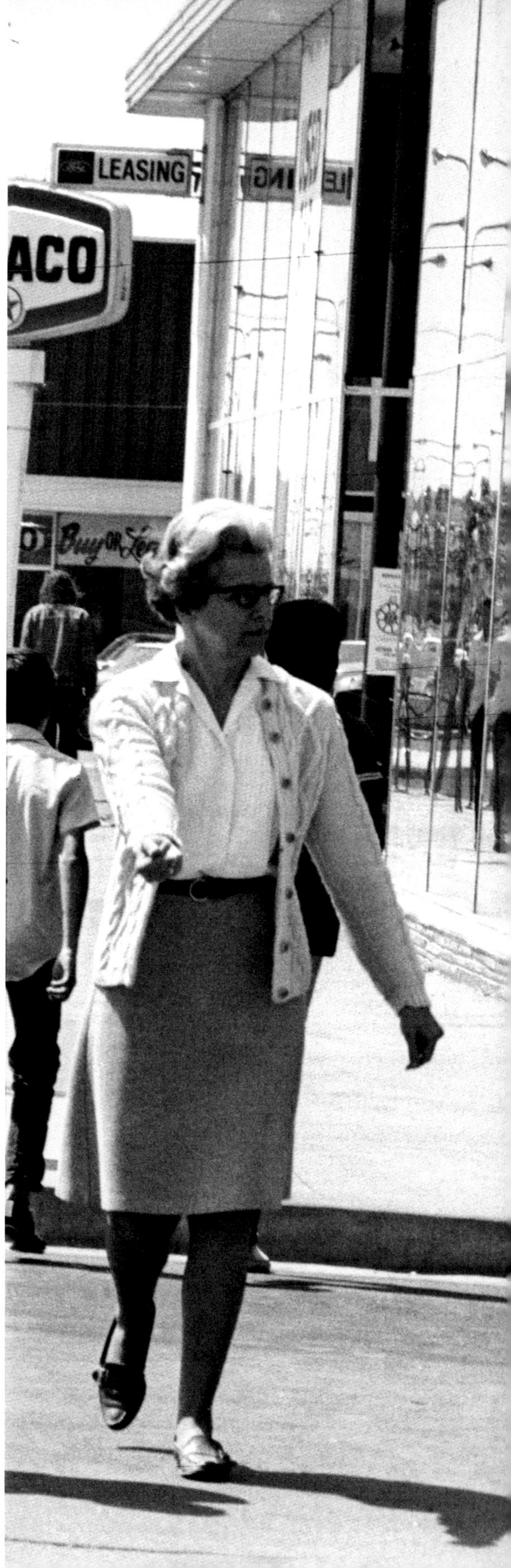


With the arrival of 2,700 National Guard troops following "Bloody Thursday," Berkeley became an occupied city.

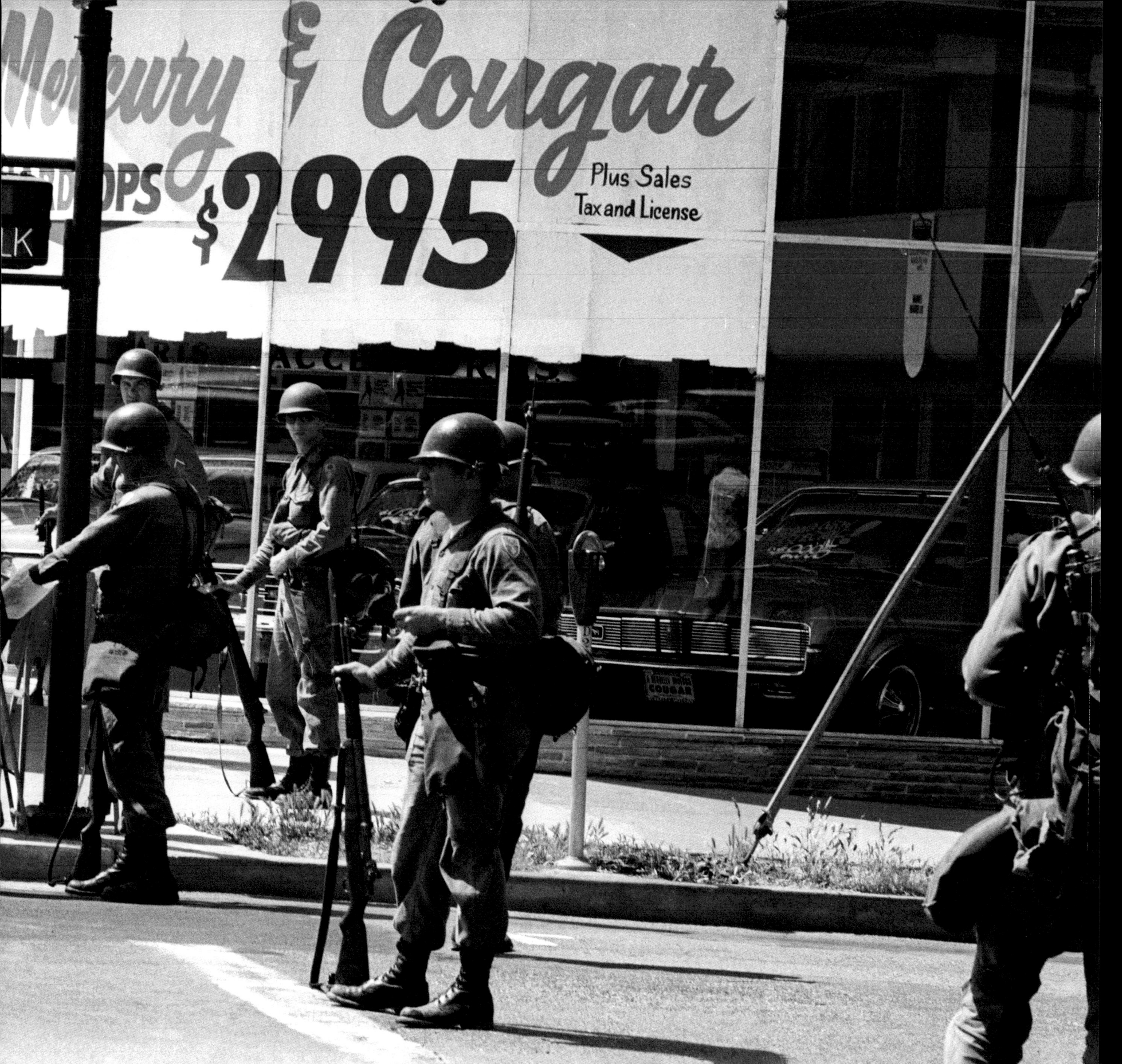

Mercury & Cougar
HARDTOPS $2995
Plus Sales
Tax and License

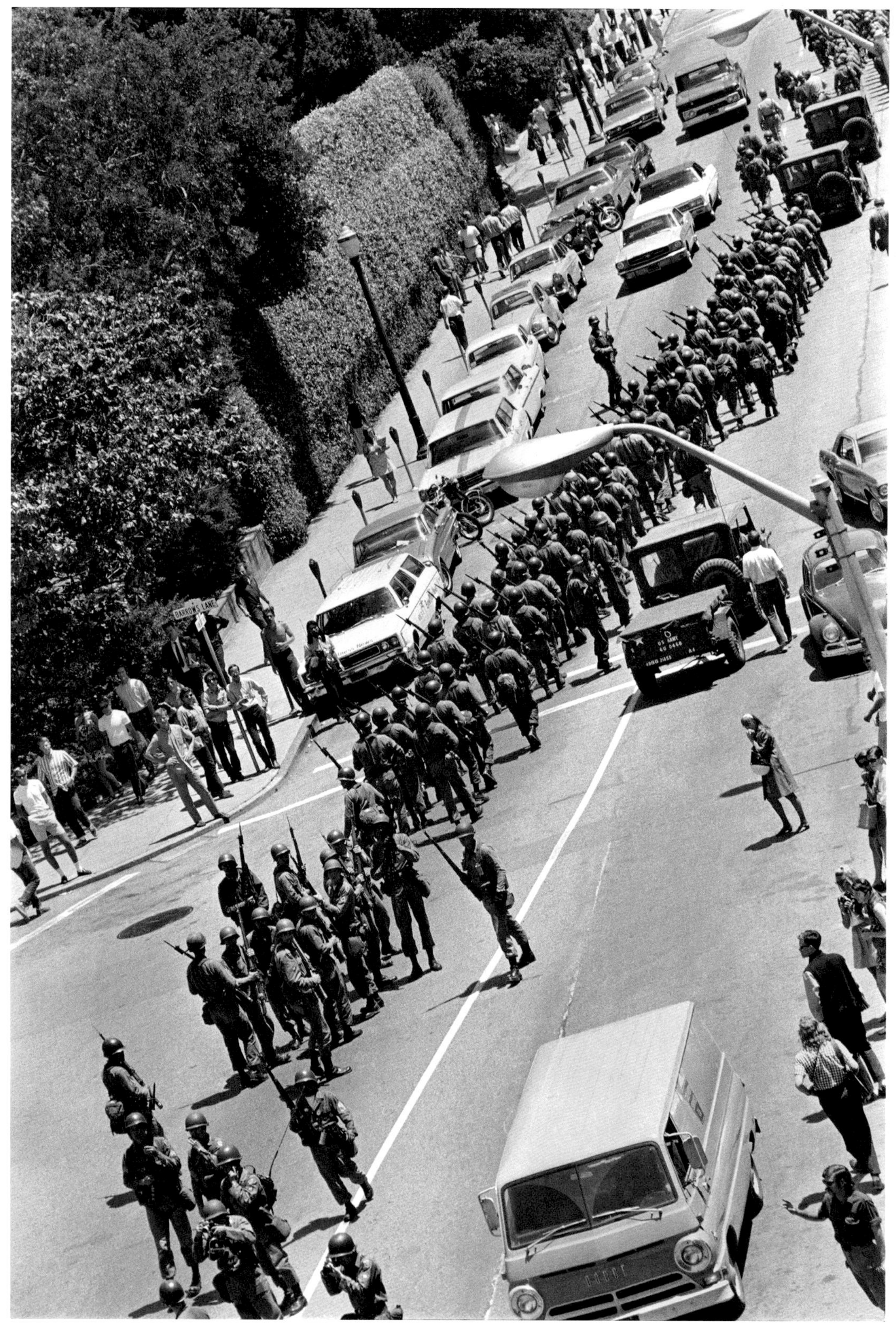

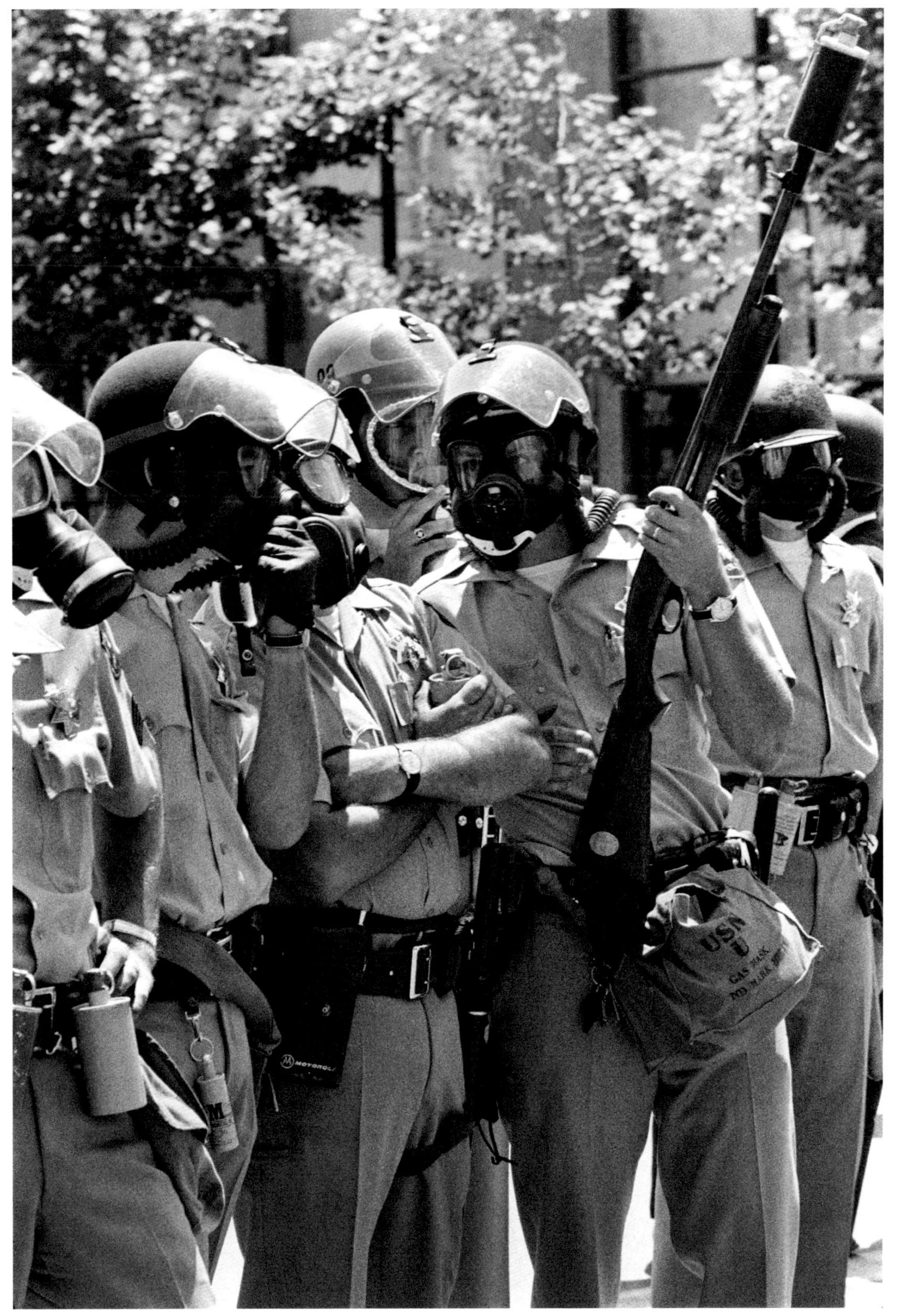

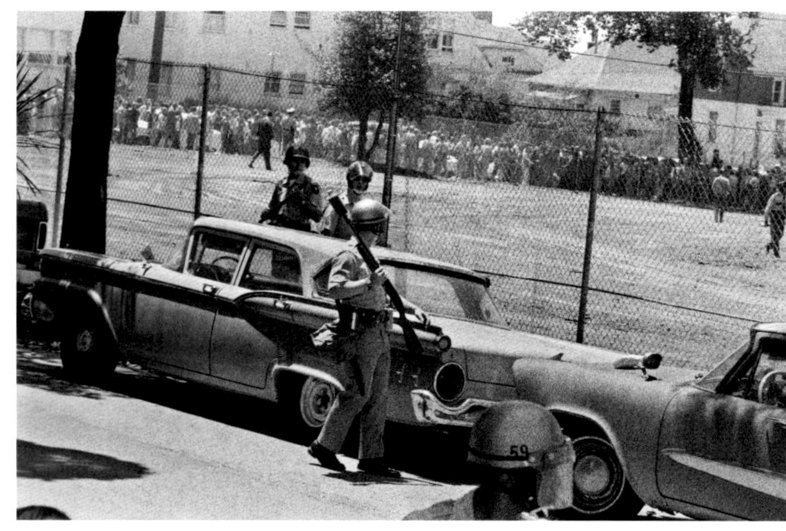

Police releasing tear gas on Haste Street alongside the fenced-off People's Park, July 14, 1969.

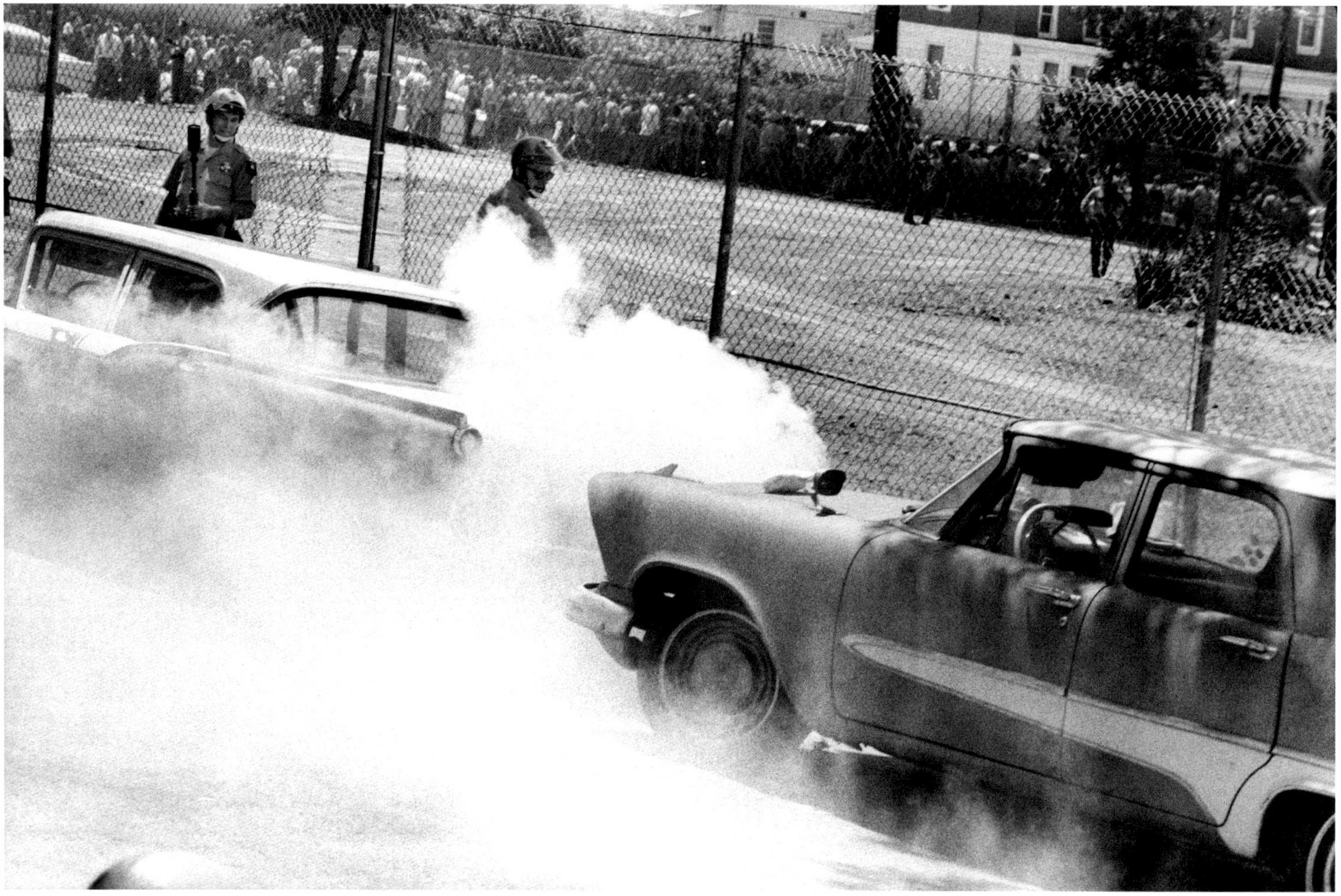

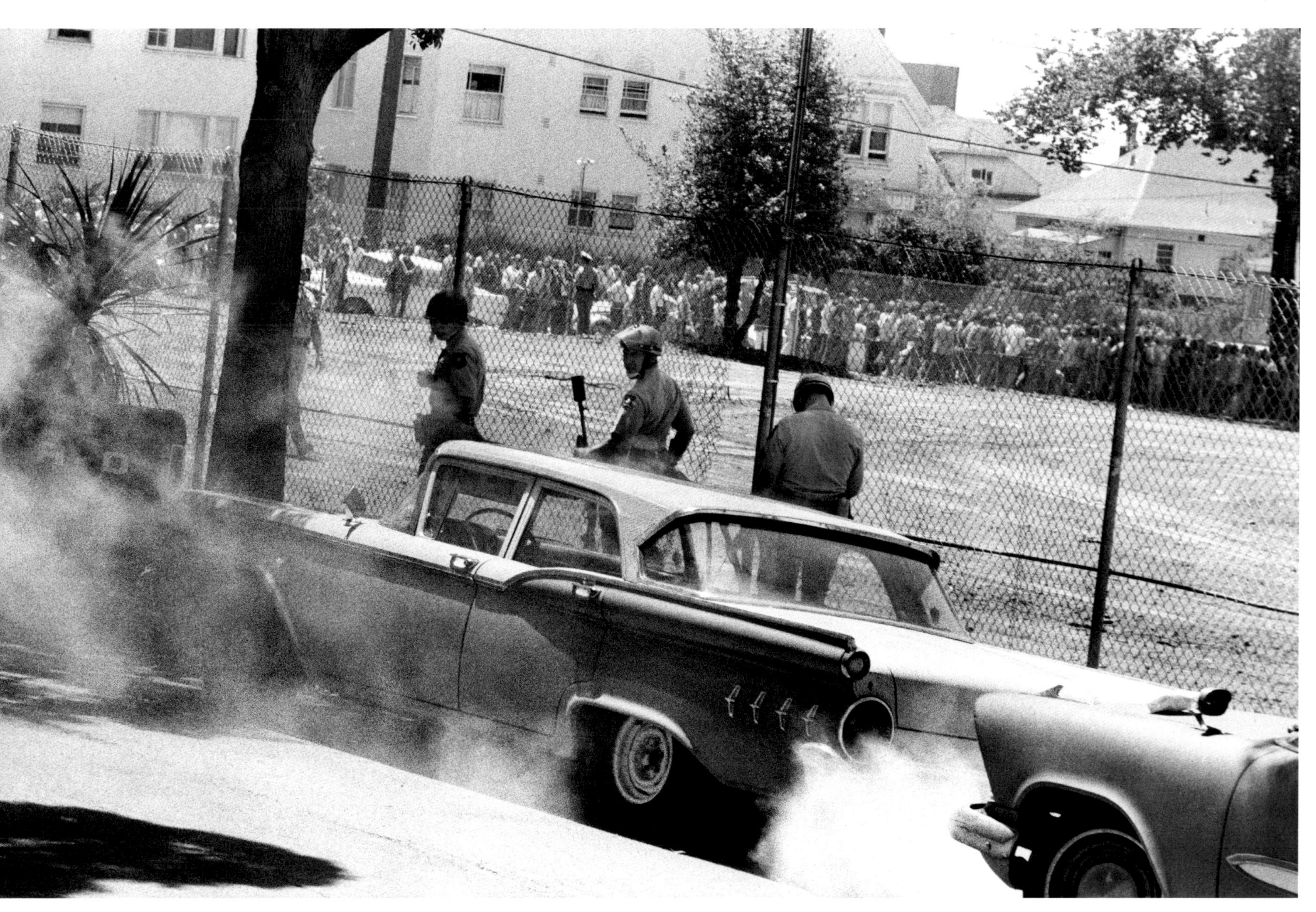

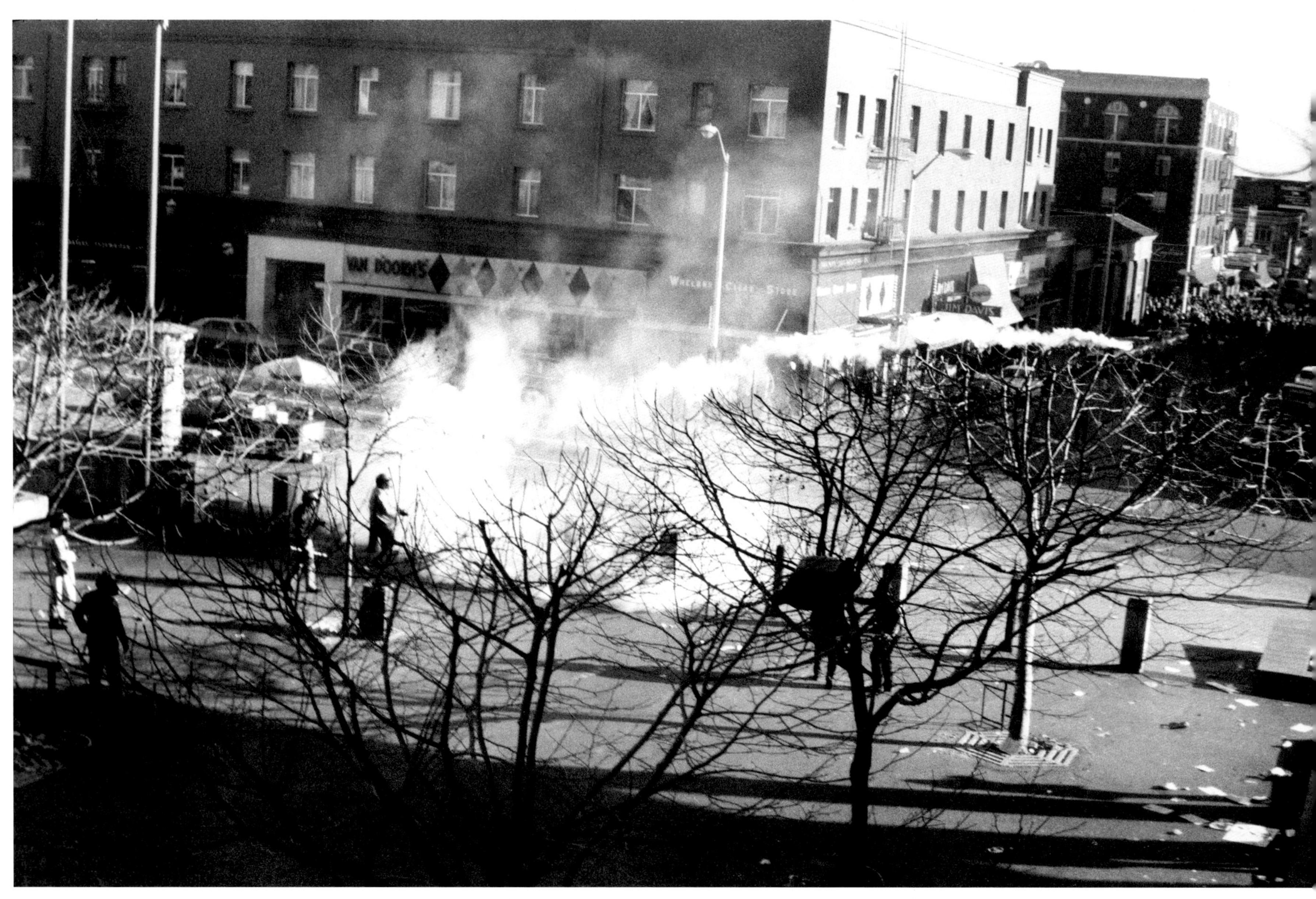

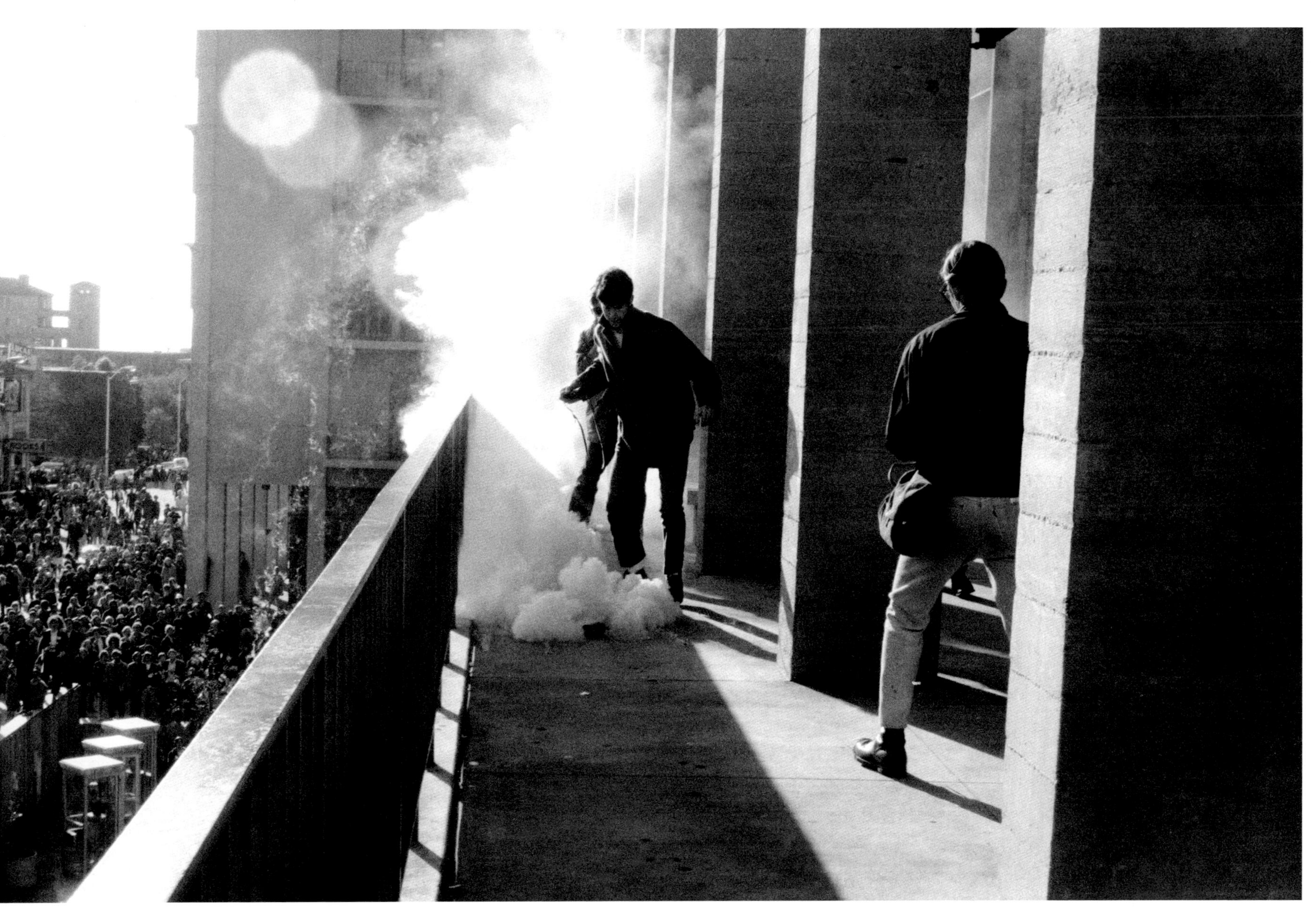

A tear gas canister landed on the balcony of the Student Union building, where people were watching a demonstration on the street below.

Panther members on guard duty behind the bus that was used as a speaker's platform at DeFremery Park alongside the old Victorian mansion there.

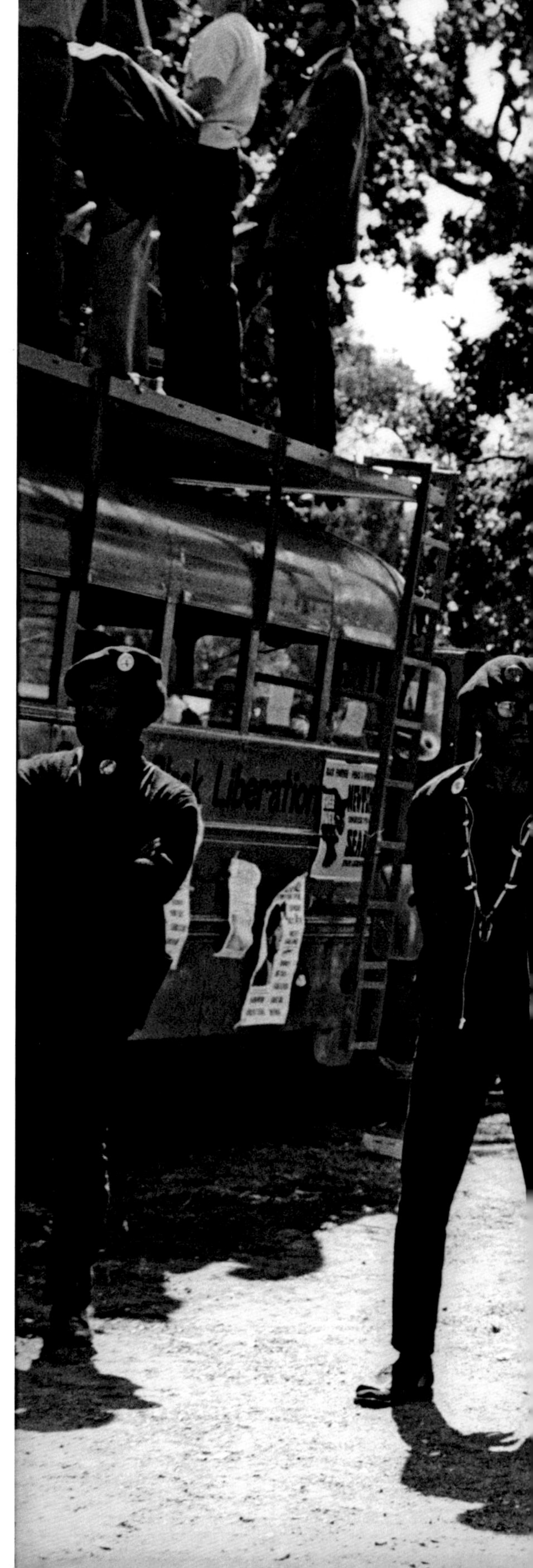

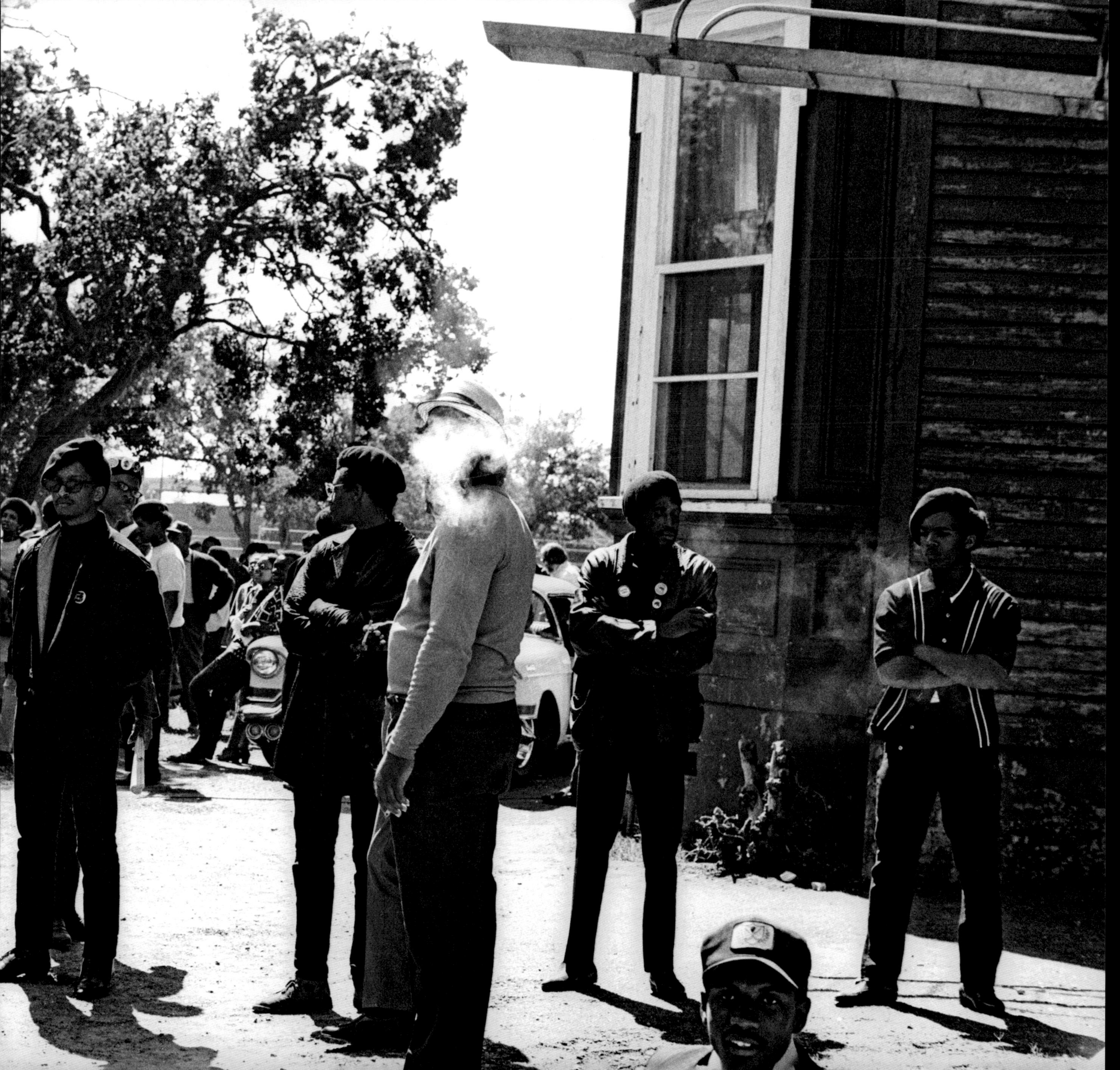

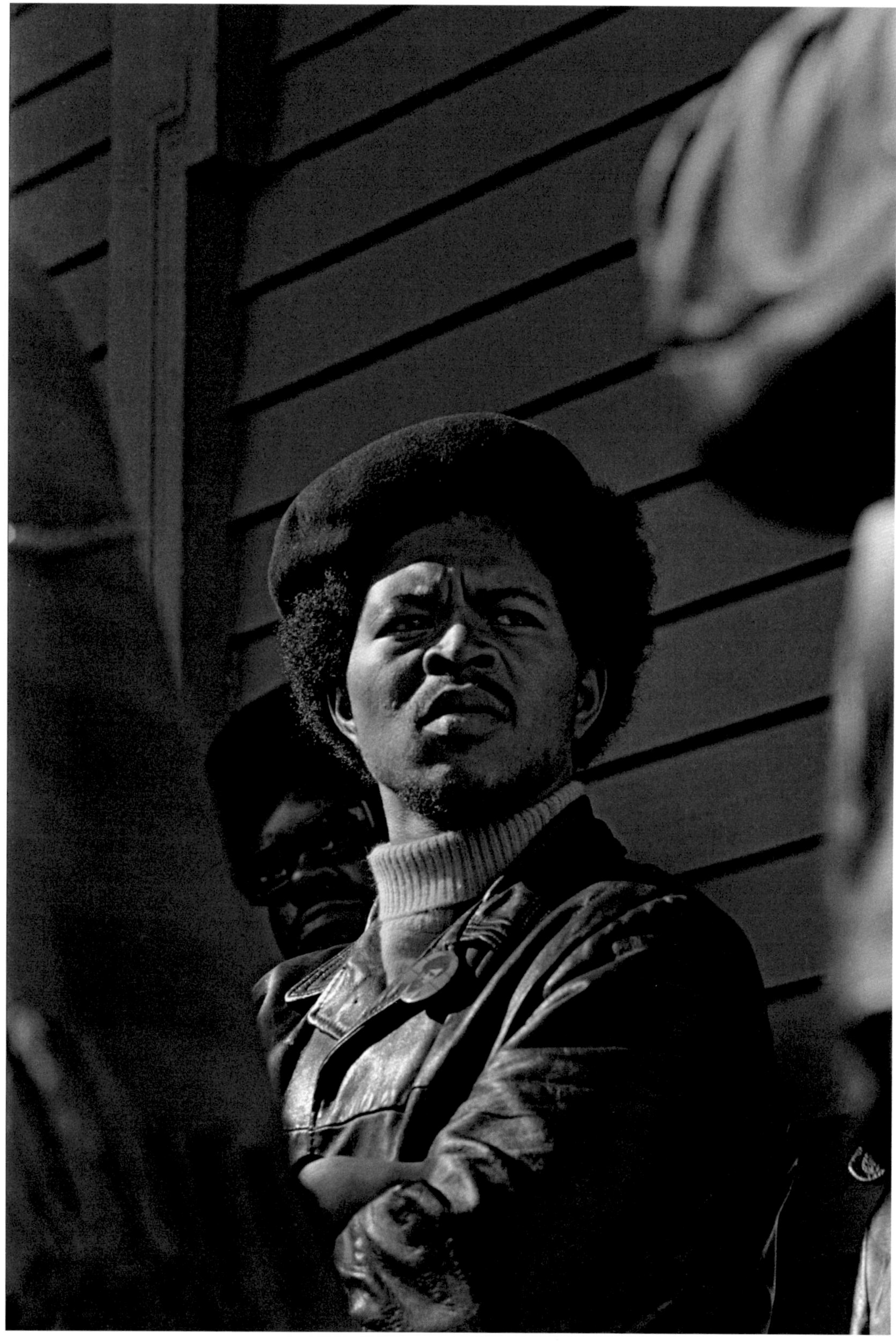

Captain Bobby Bowens of the Panthers' Richmond, California chapter at a Free Huey rally at DeFremery Park.

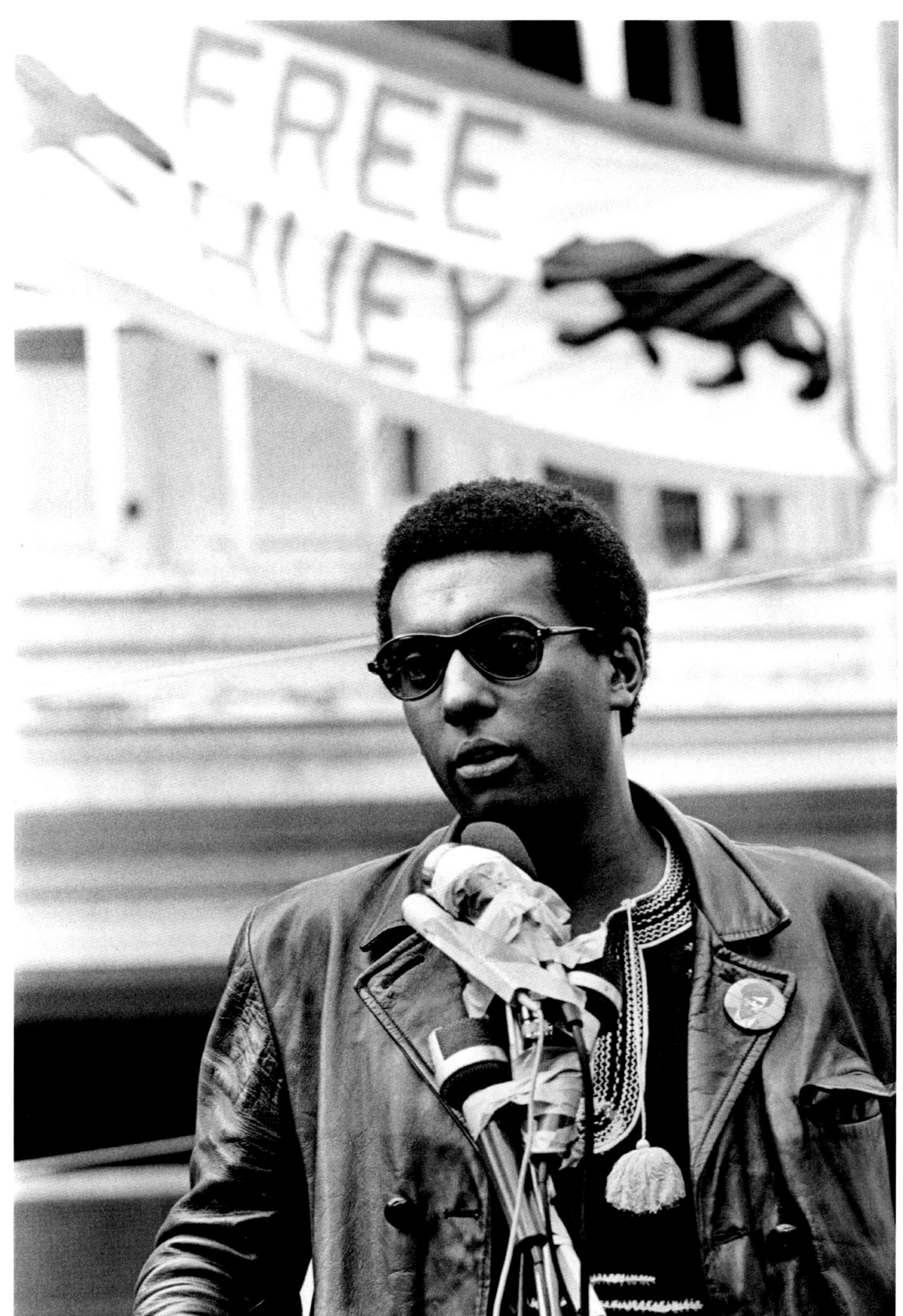



Stokely Carmichael
at a Free Huey rally,
August 25, 1968, at
DeFremery Park.

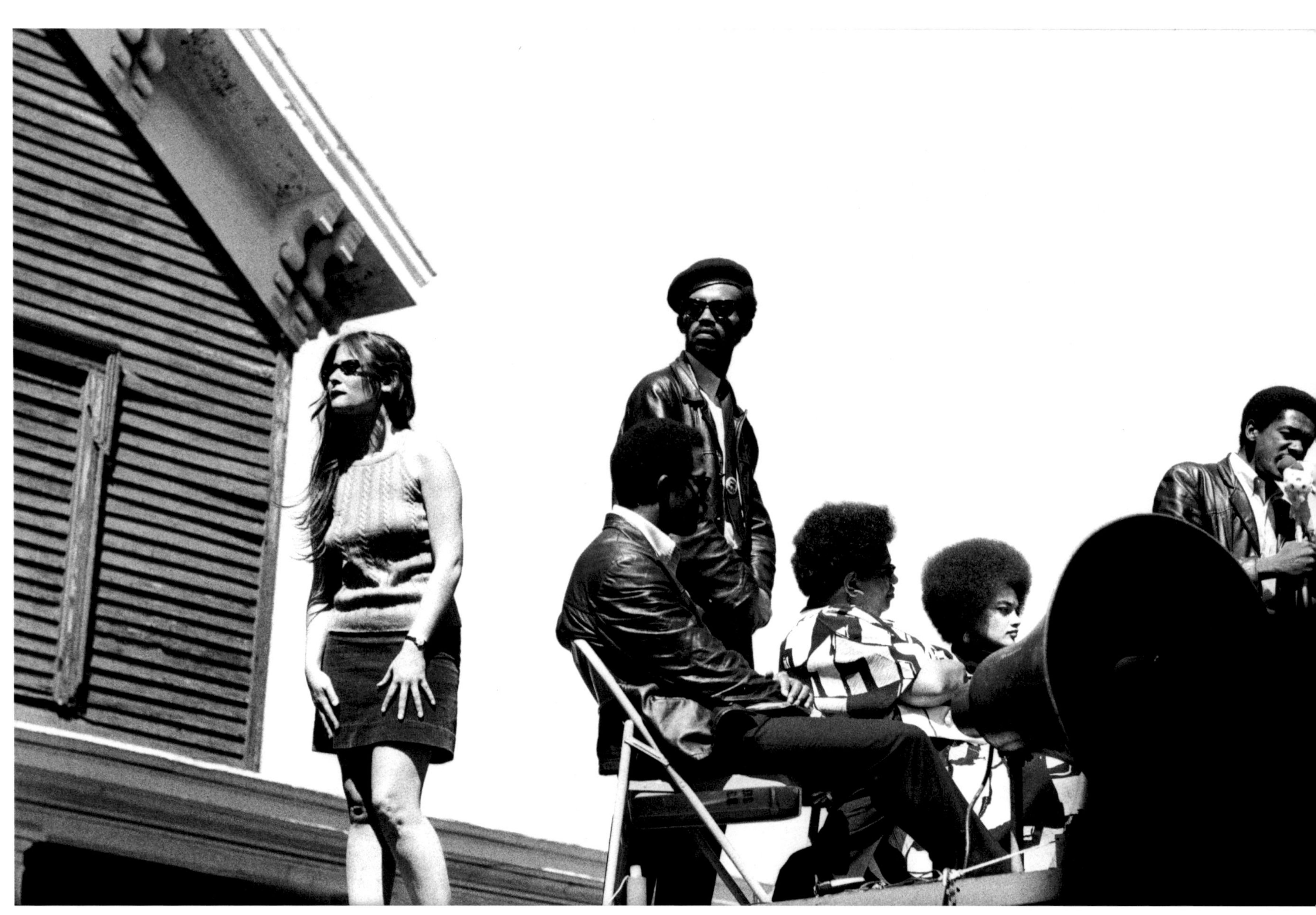

On the bus used as a speaker's platform at the park, Eldridge Cleaver, Ruth Hagwood and Kathleen Cleaver listen as Bobby Seale speaks to supporters.

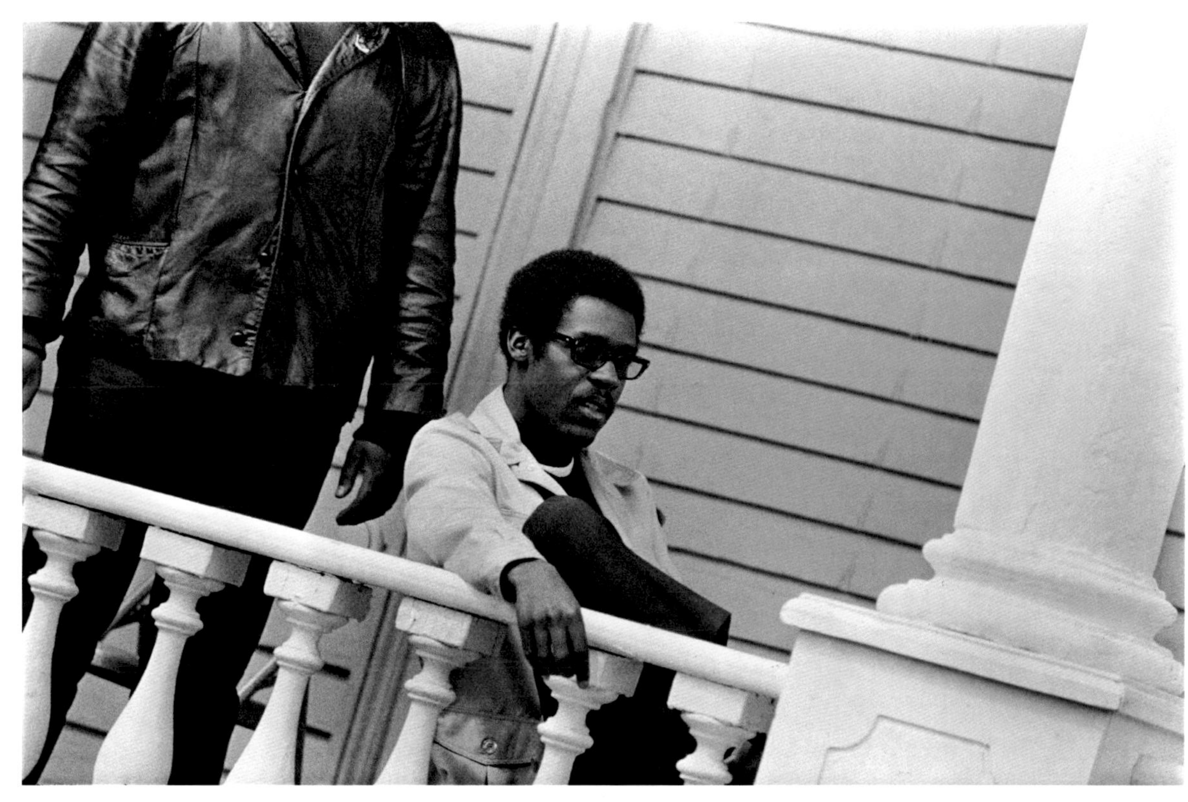

Panther Chief of Staff David Hilliard, left, and Bobby Seale, below, with June Hilliard during rallies at DeFremery Park.

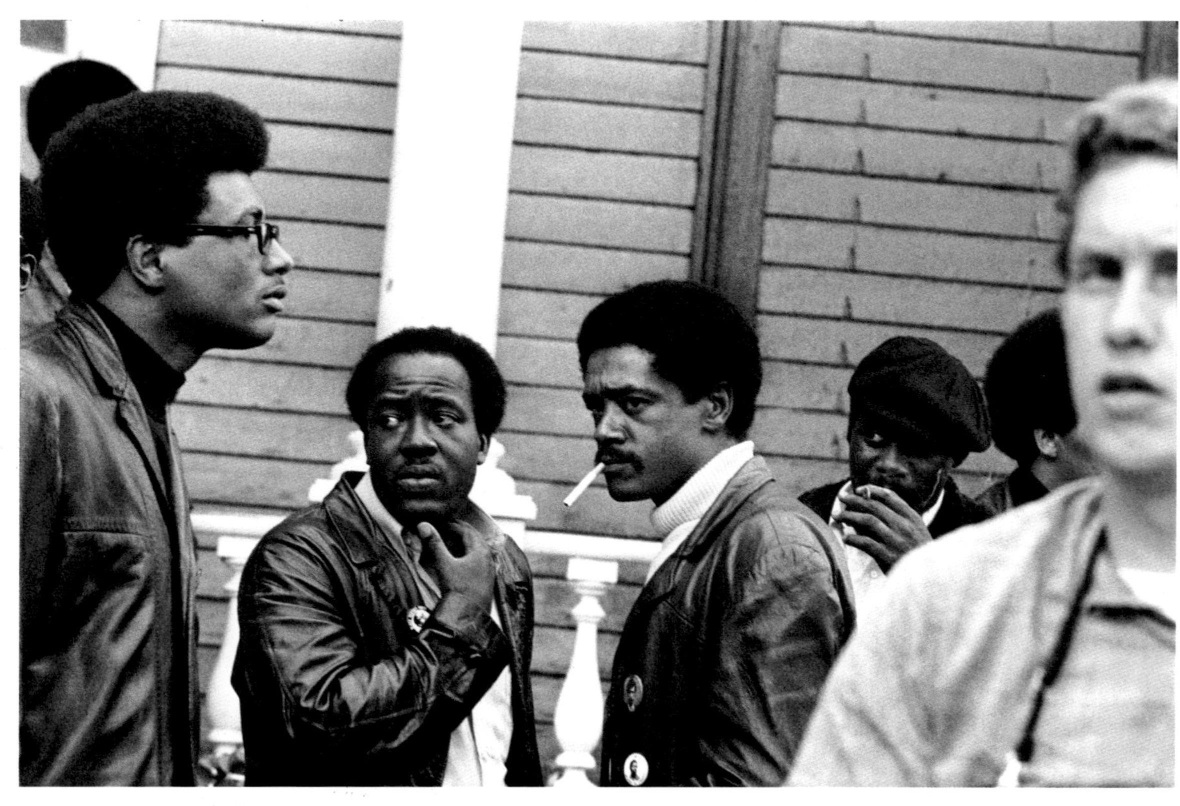

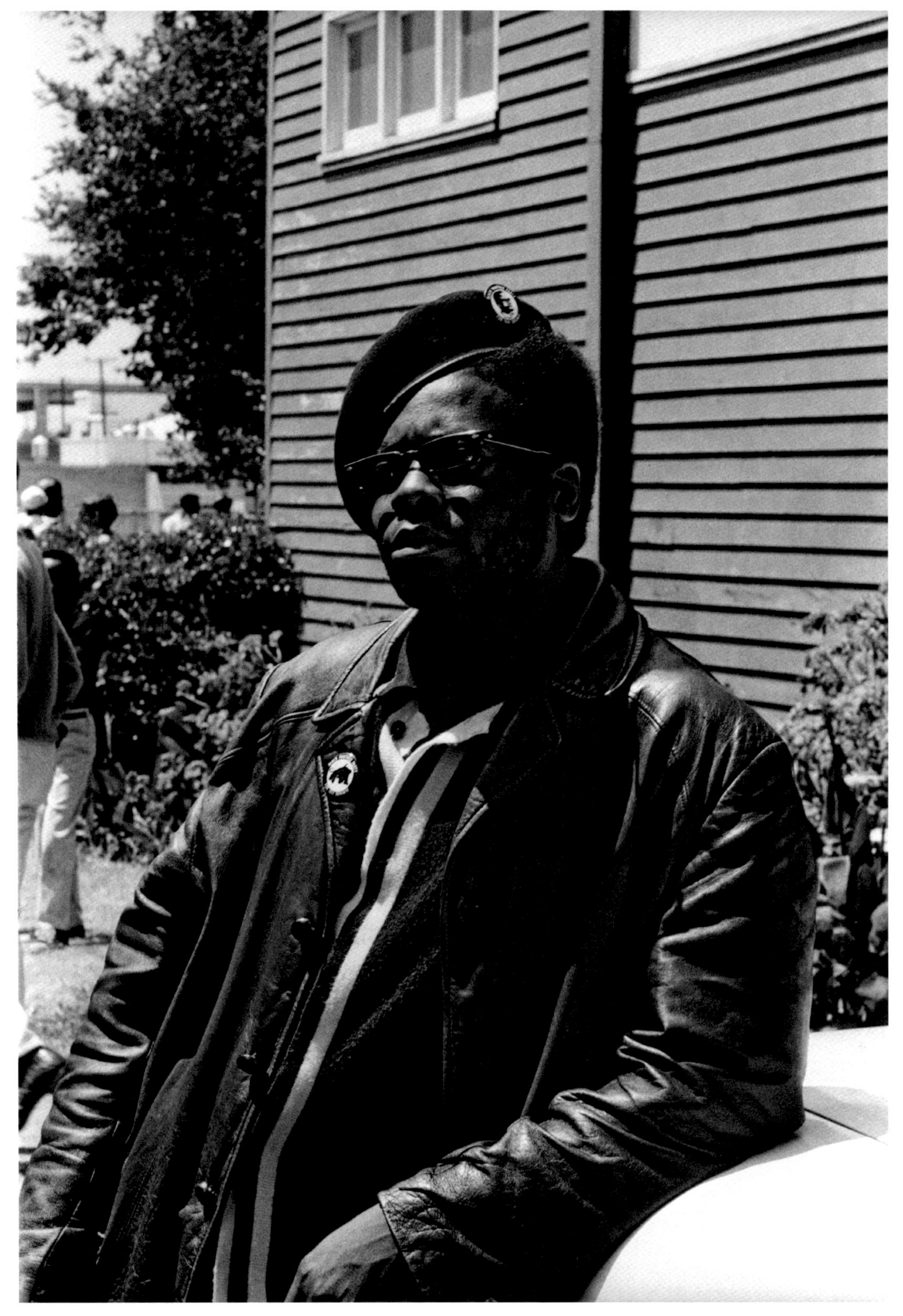

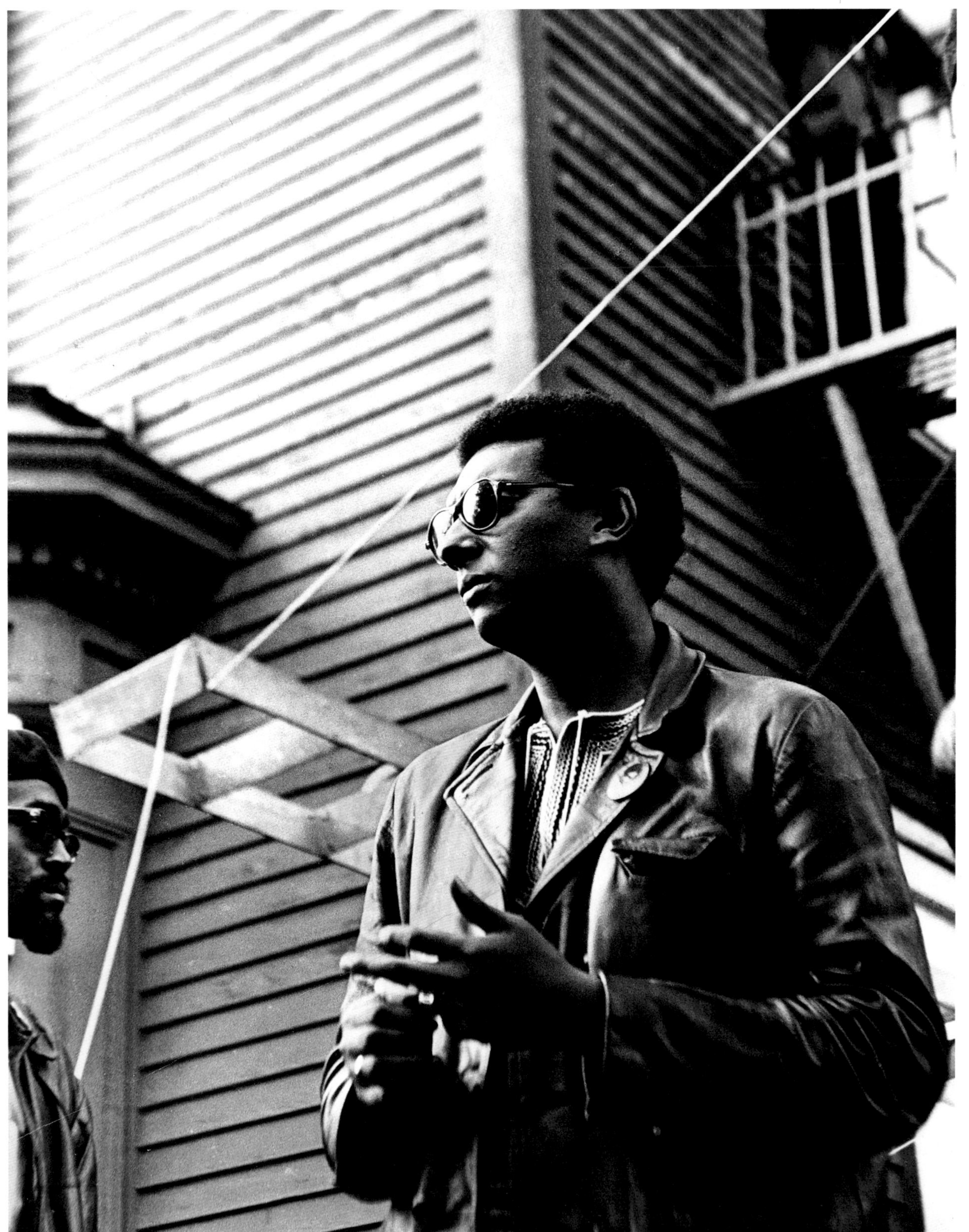

okely Carmichael,
ht, and Panther
mber "Boston,"
posite, at the park.

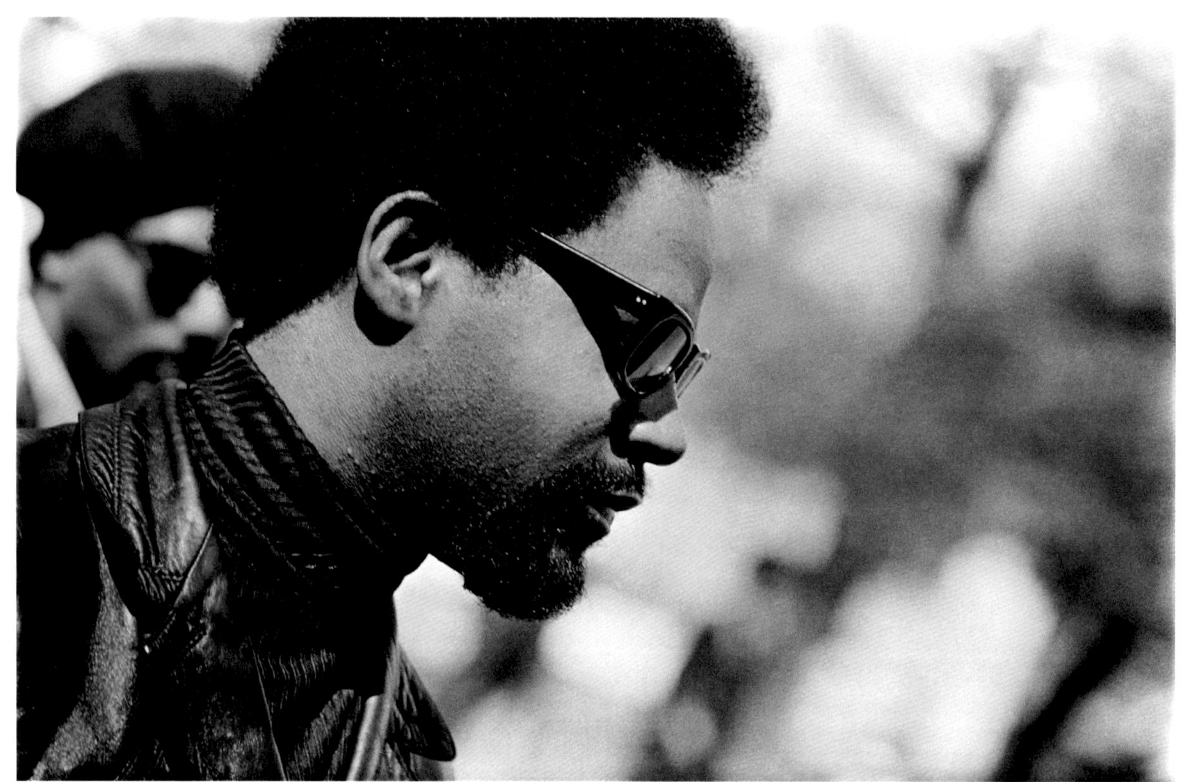

Emory Douglas, Minis
of Culture for the
Black Panther Party, a
DeFremery Park.

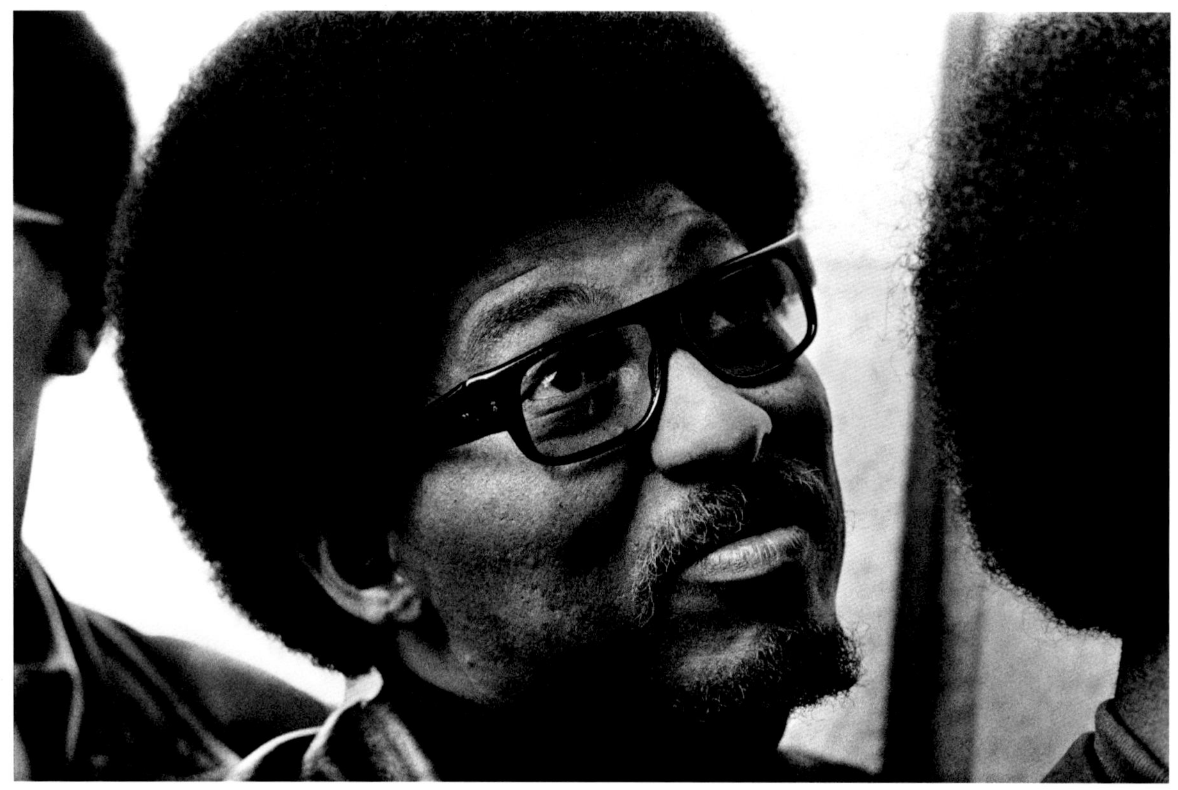

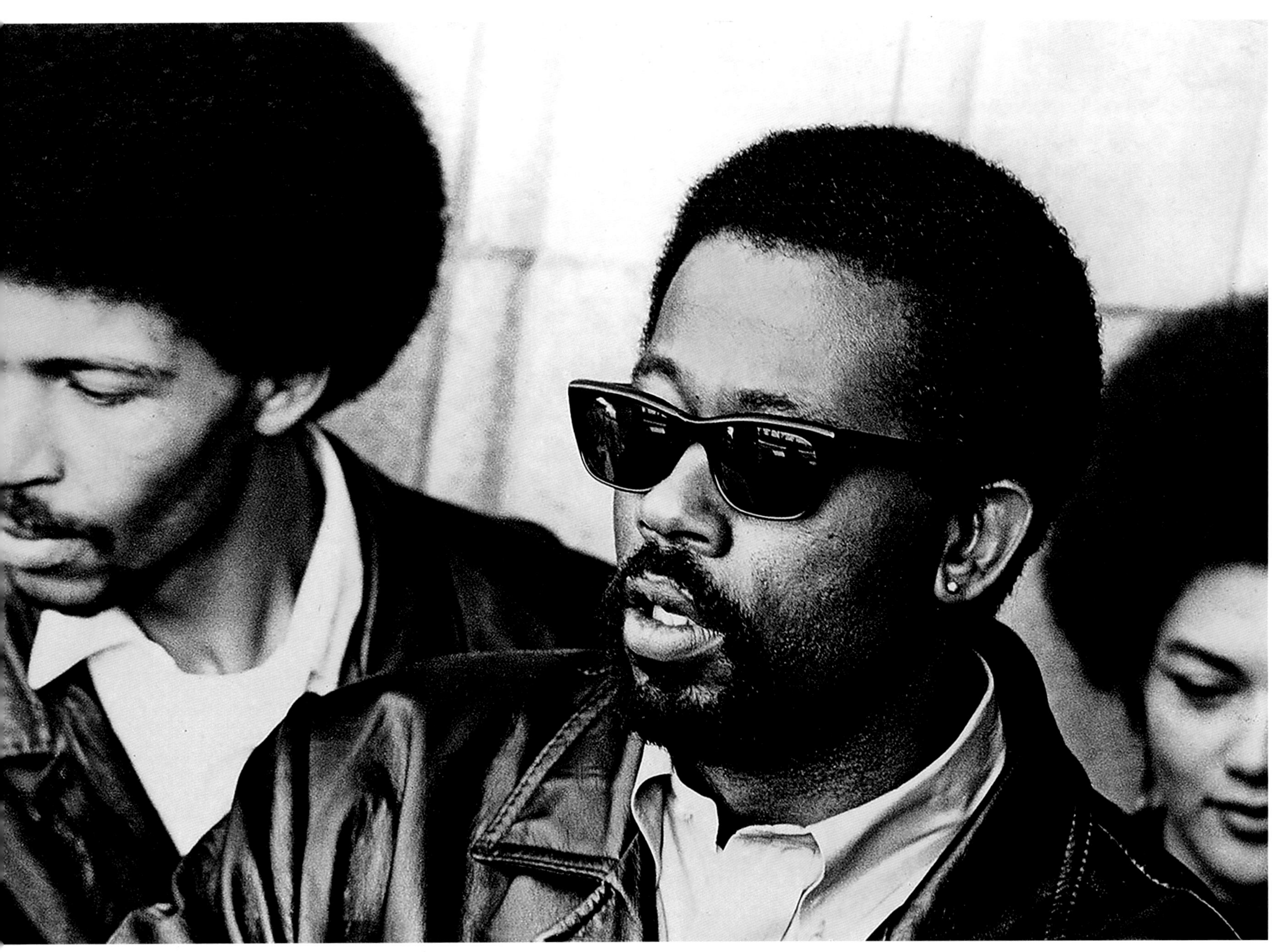

Waiting in line to attend the trial of Huey Newton at the Alameda County Courthouse. Above, Eldridge Cleaver and opposite, Donald "DC" Cox.

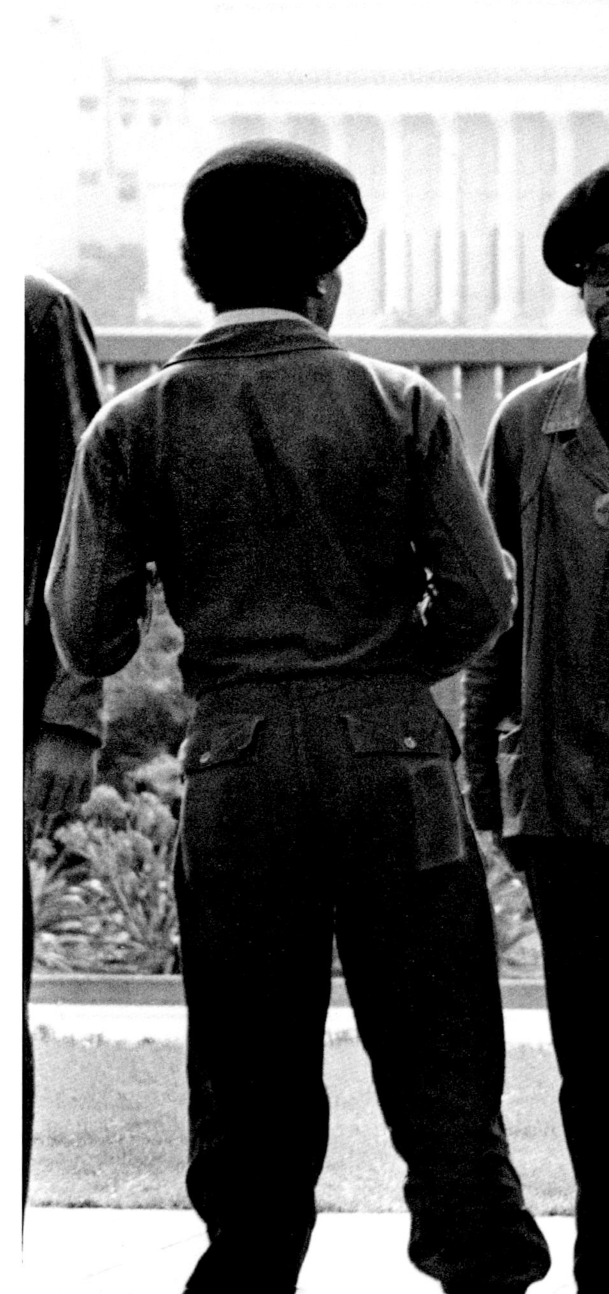

Elbert "Big Man" Howard, center, with other Panthers near a bust of Abraham Lincoln at the Alameda County Courthouse.

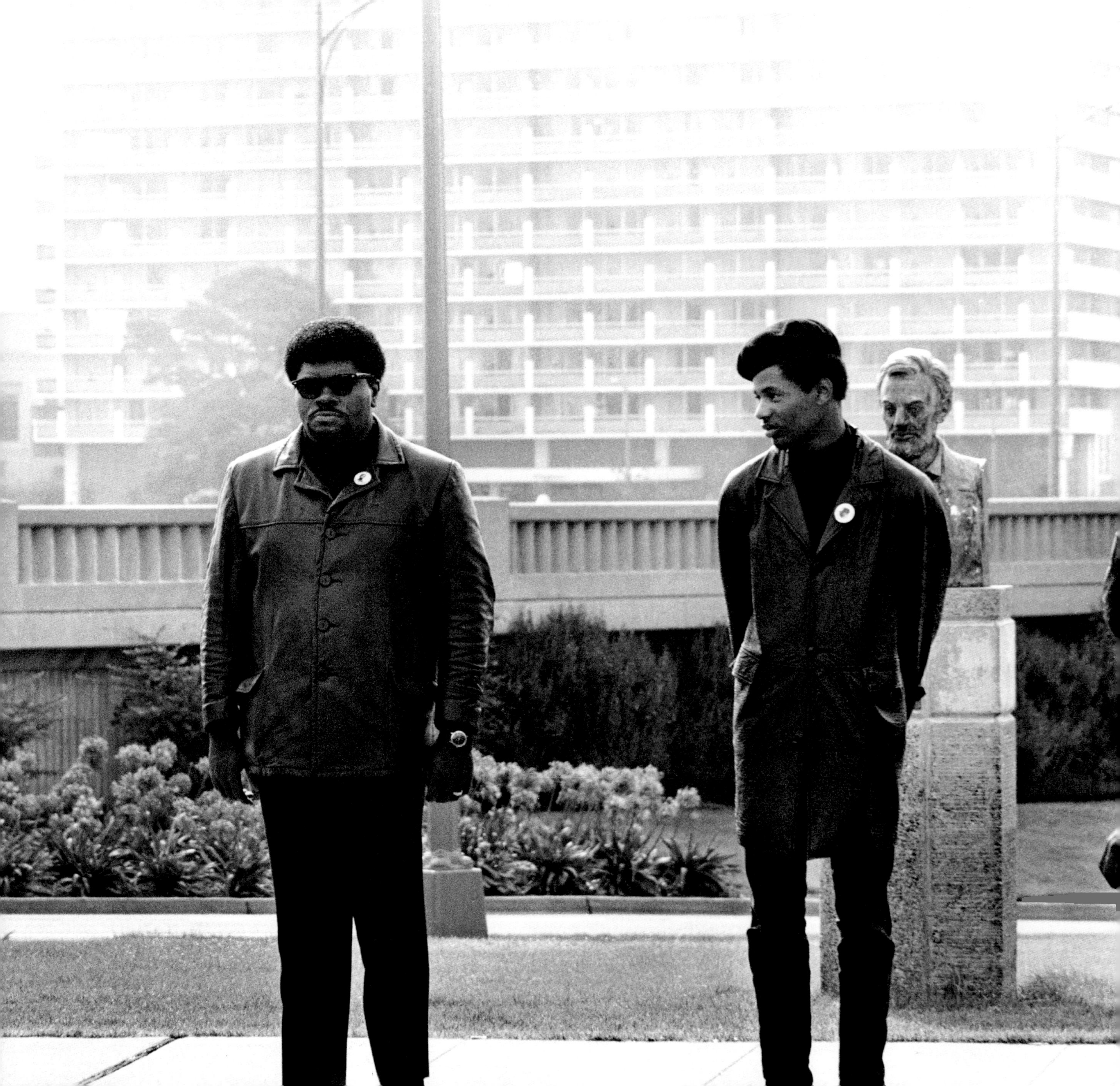

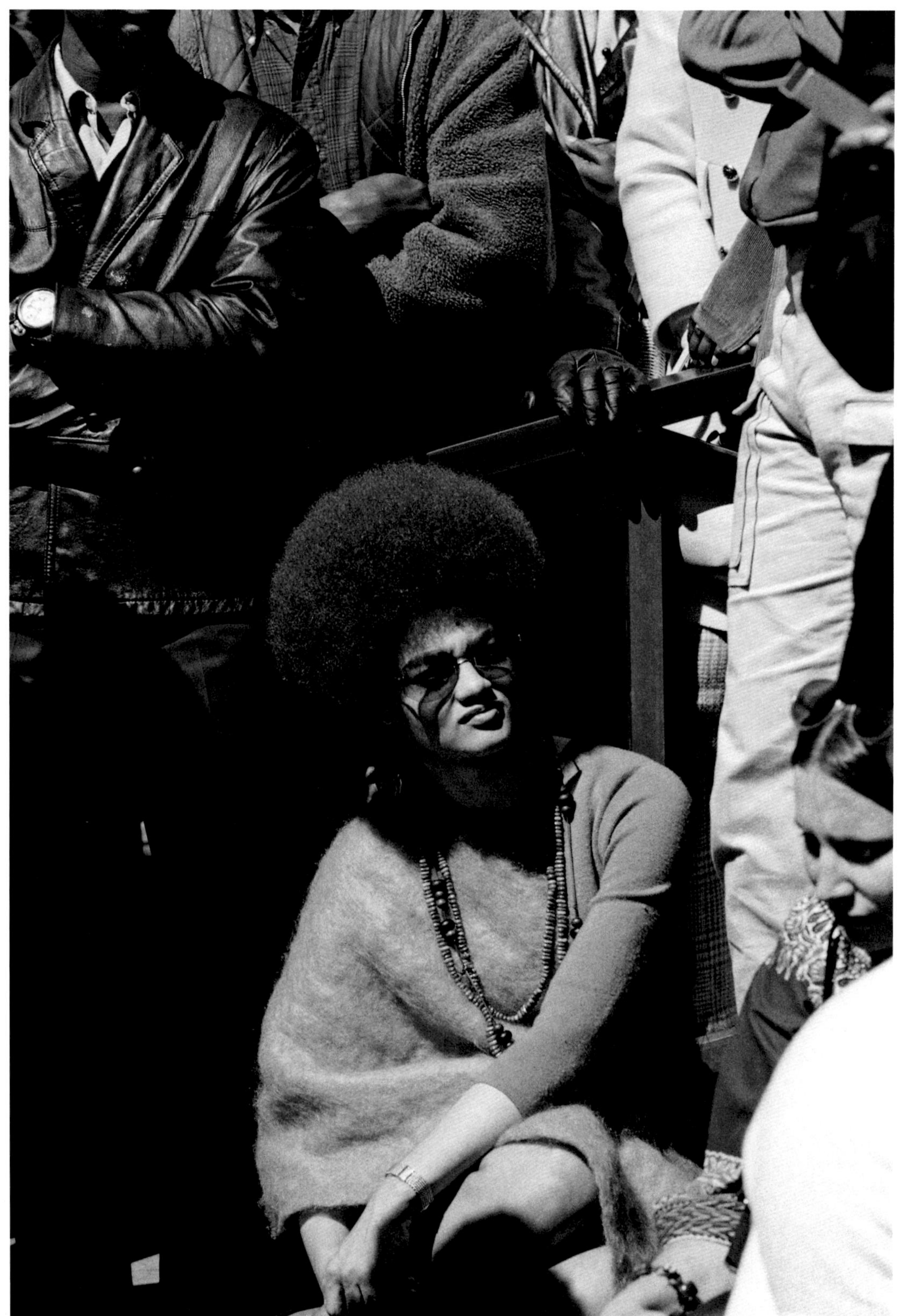

Kathleen Cleaver, National Communications Secretary of the Panthers, at a May Day rally to free Huey Newton at the Federal Building in San Francisco, 1969.

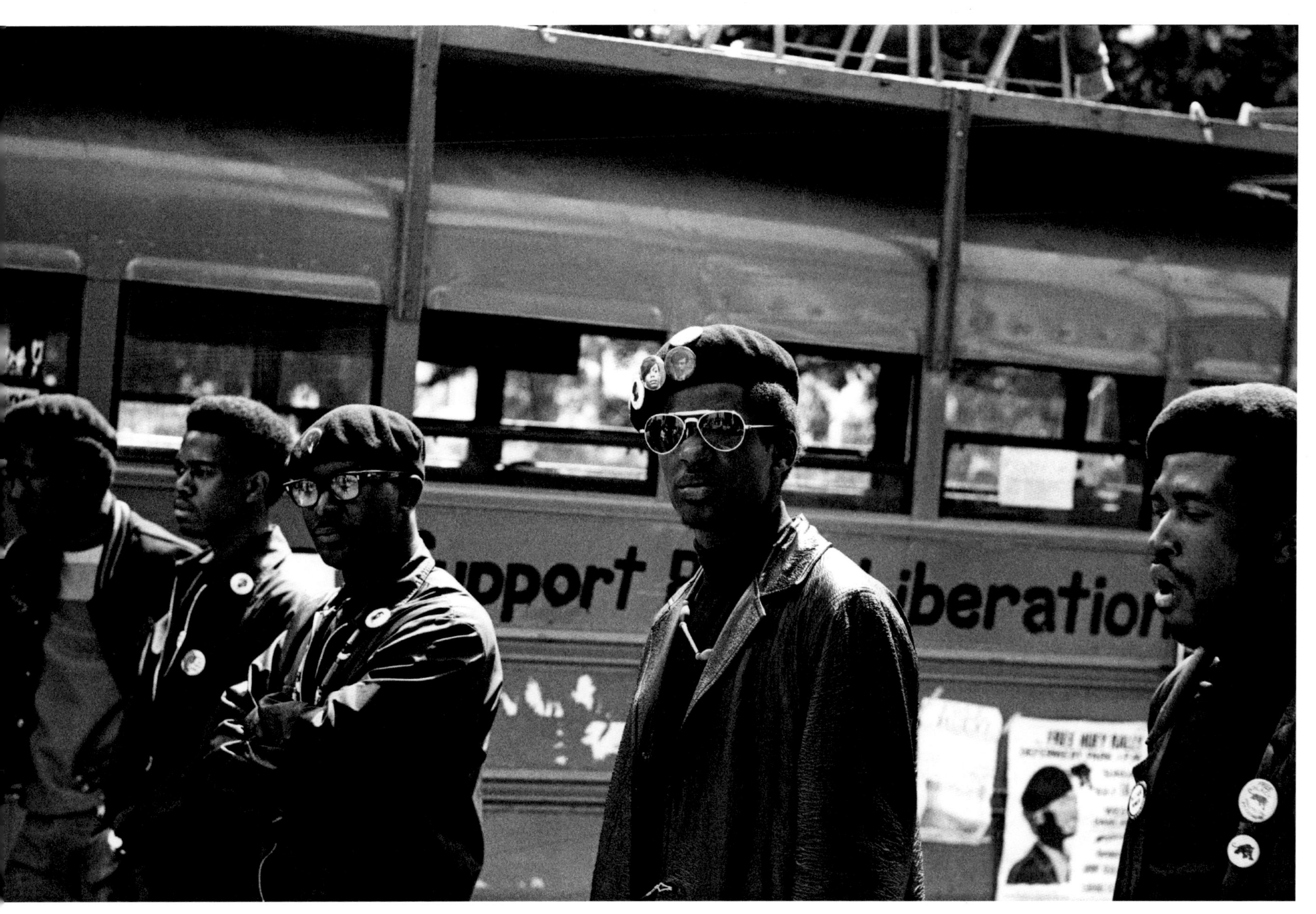

Black Panther security at DeFremery Park.

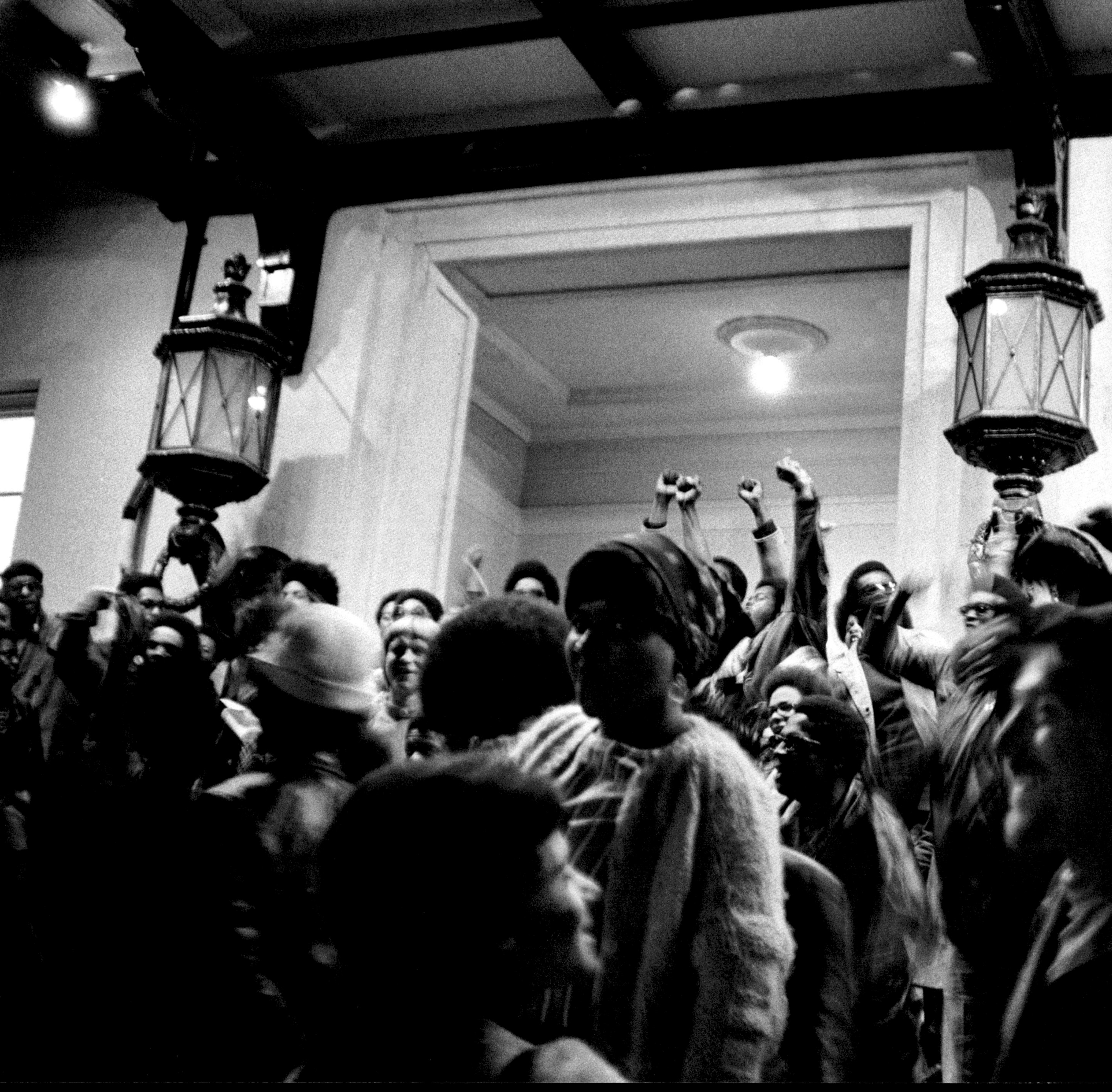

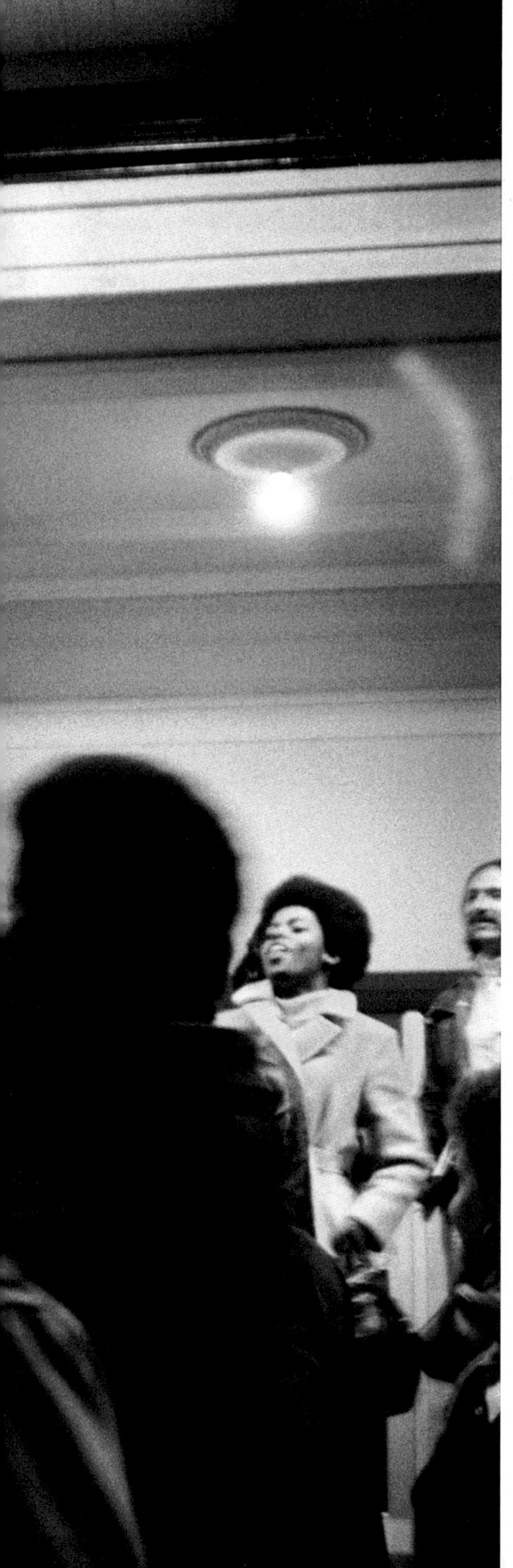

Judging by the many rolls of film I shot in July 1969 of a Panther event that began on my 15th birthday, I was beginning to work like a professional documentary photographer. The three-day Revolutionary Conference for a United Front Against Fascism, at the Oakland Auditorium, emphasized the Panthers' desire for multiracial unity of purpose with a program of speakers and workshops to address the needs of all poor, oppressed workers and people of America. The Panthers highlighted the links between police violence in communities of color, the movement to free Huey Newton and the police violence during demonstrations over People's Park that had taken place earlier that year.

Outside the conference at the Oakland Auditorium, July 1969.

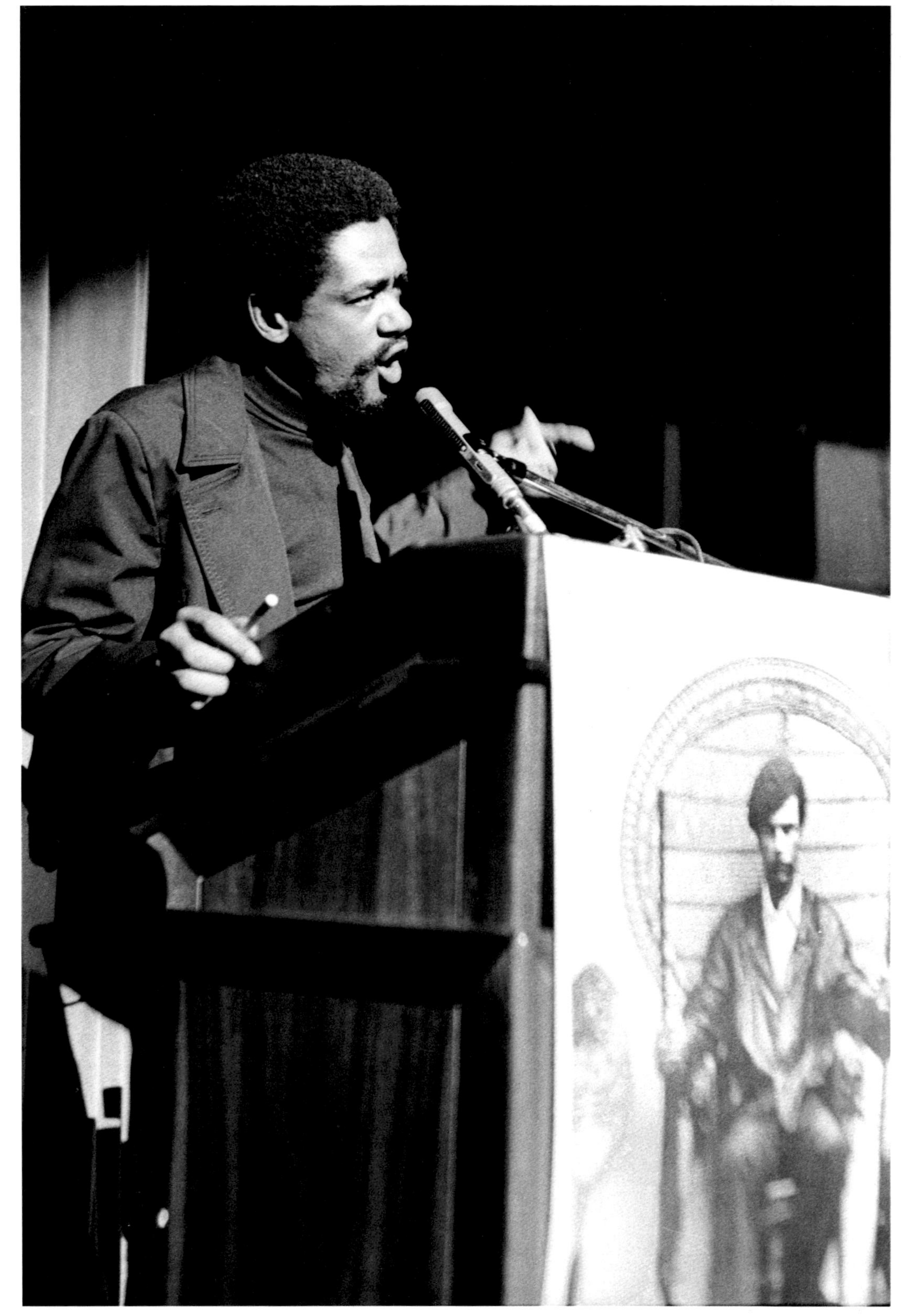

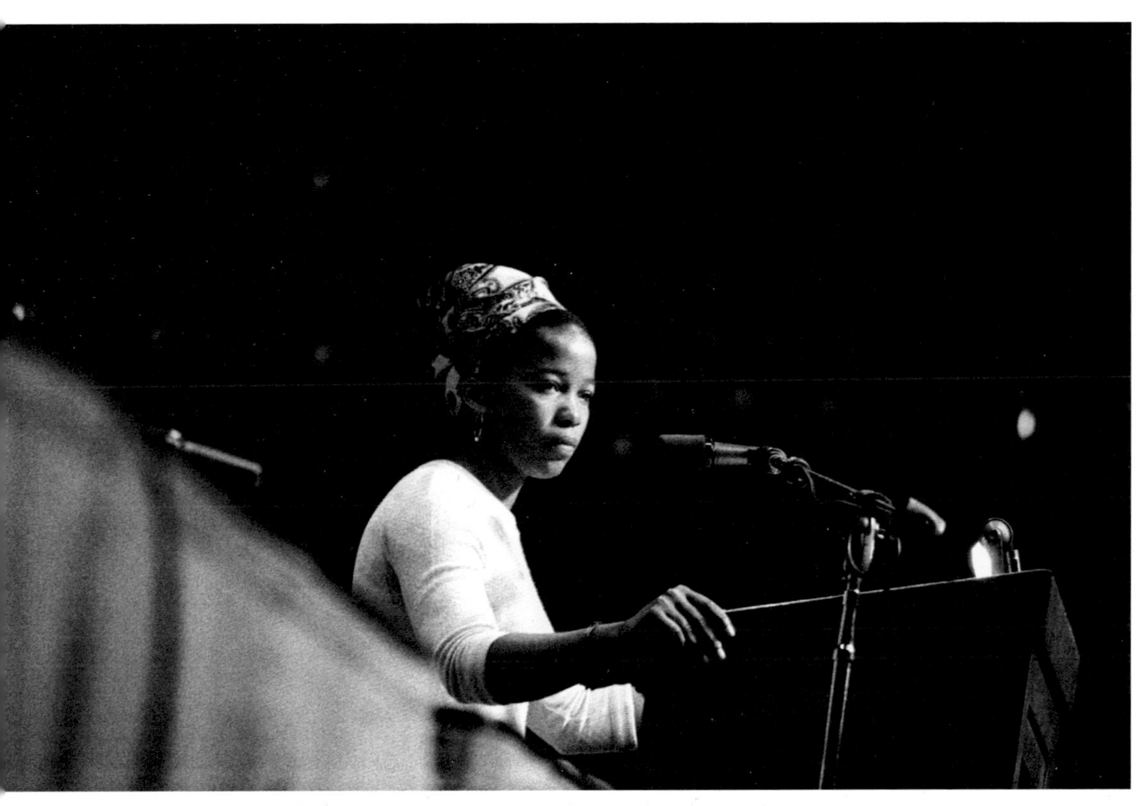

oby Seale, opposite, at a rally in 1969.
...ther Carol Henry, above, and Ducho
...nnis, right, official Panther photographer
...d union organizer at the United Front
...ainst Fascism conference.

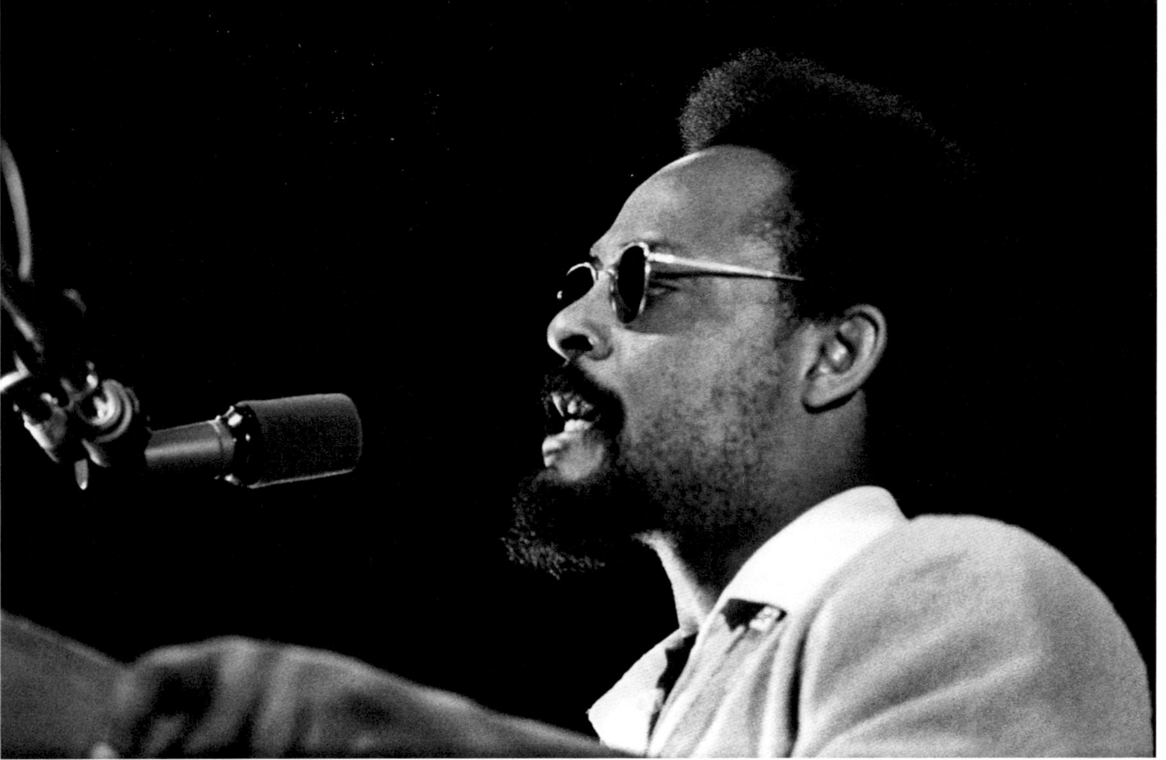

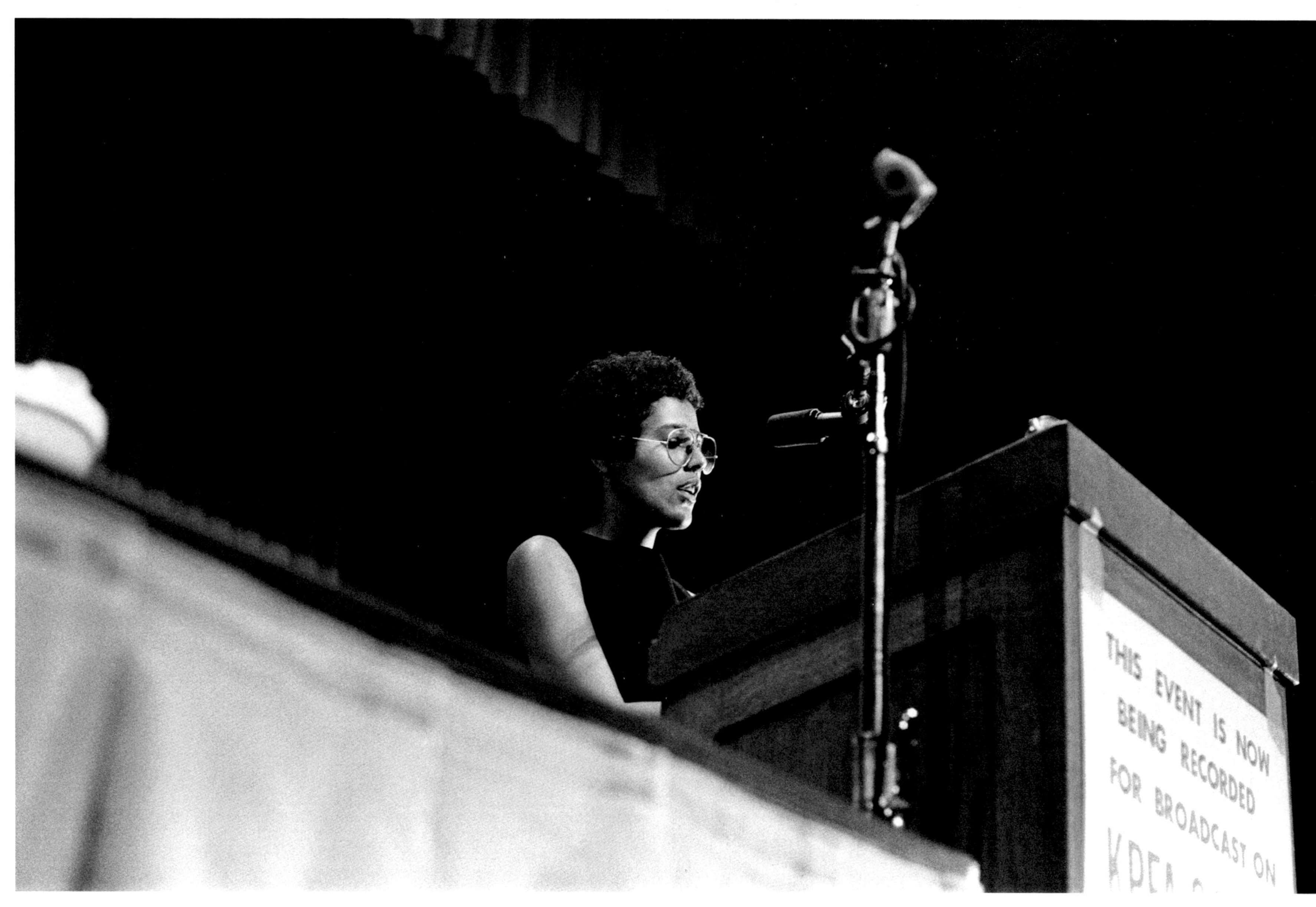


Leading Black Panther Party member Elaine Brown, who was eventually named chairwoman, reading a statement by then-imprisoned New Haven Panther member Ericka Huggins at the United Front Against Fascism conference.

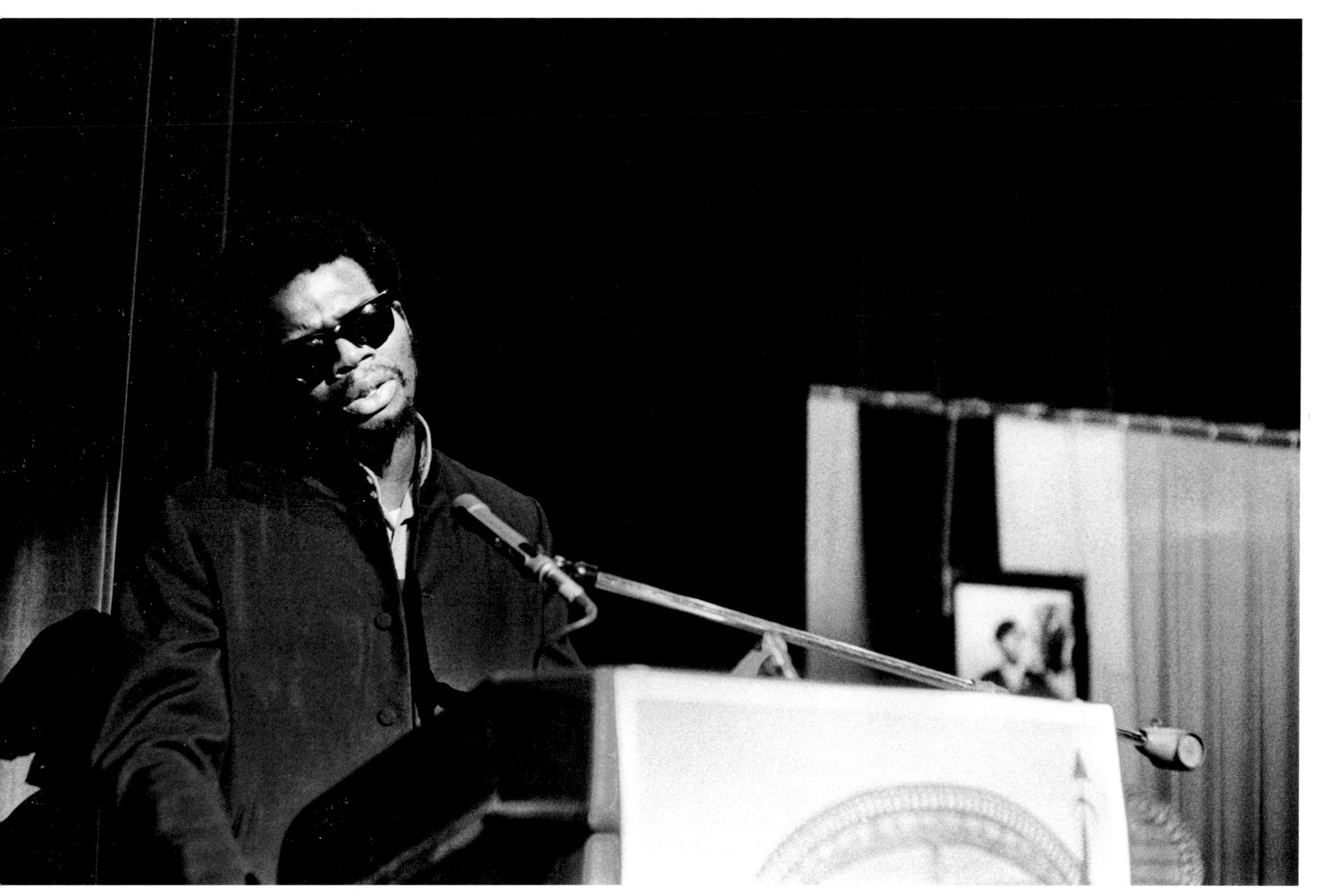

George Murray, former Black Panther Minister
of Education, at a rally in 1969.

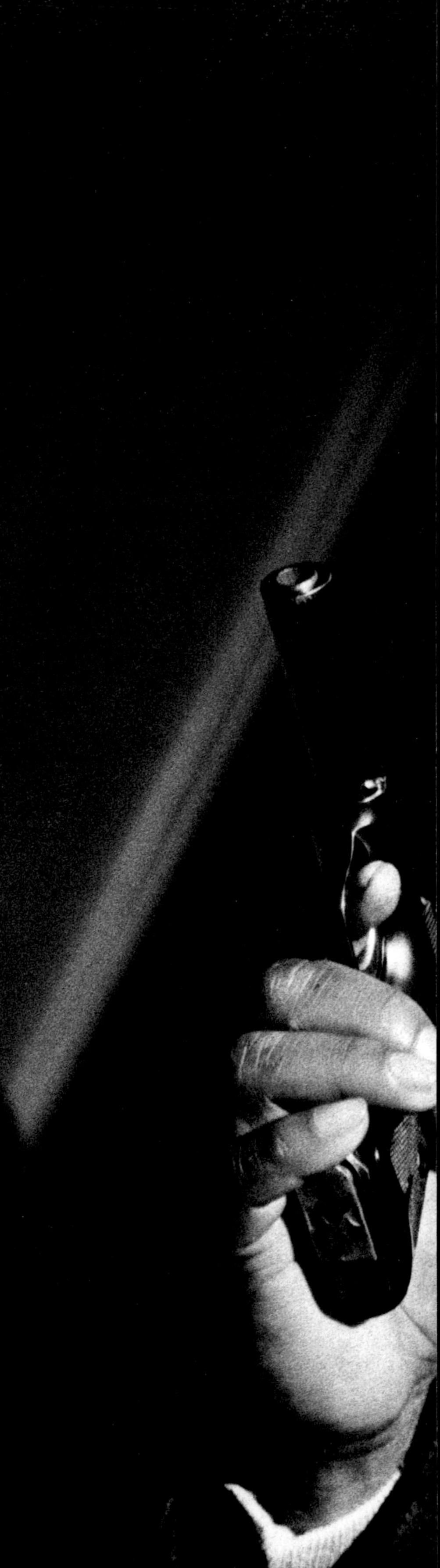

George "Baby D" Gains, Captain of the Marin Panther chapter, addressing a rally in 1969.

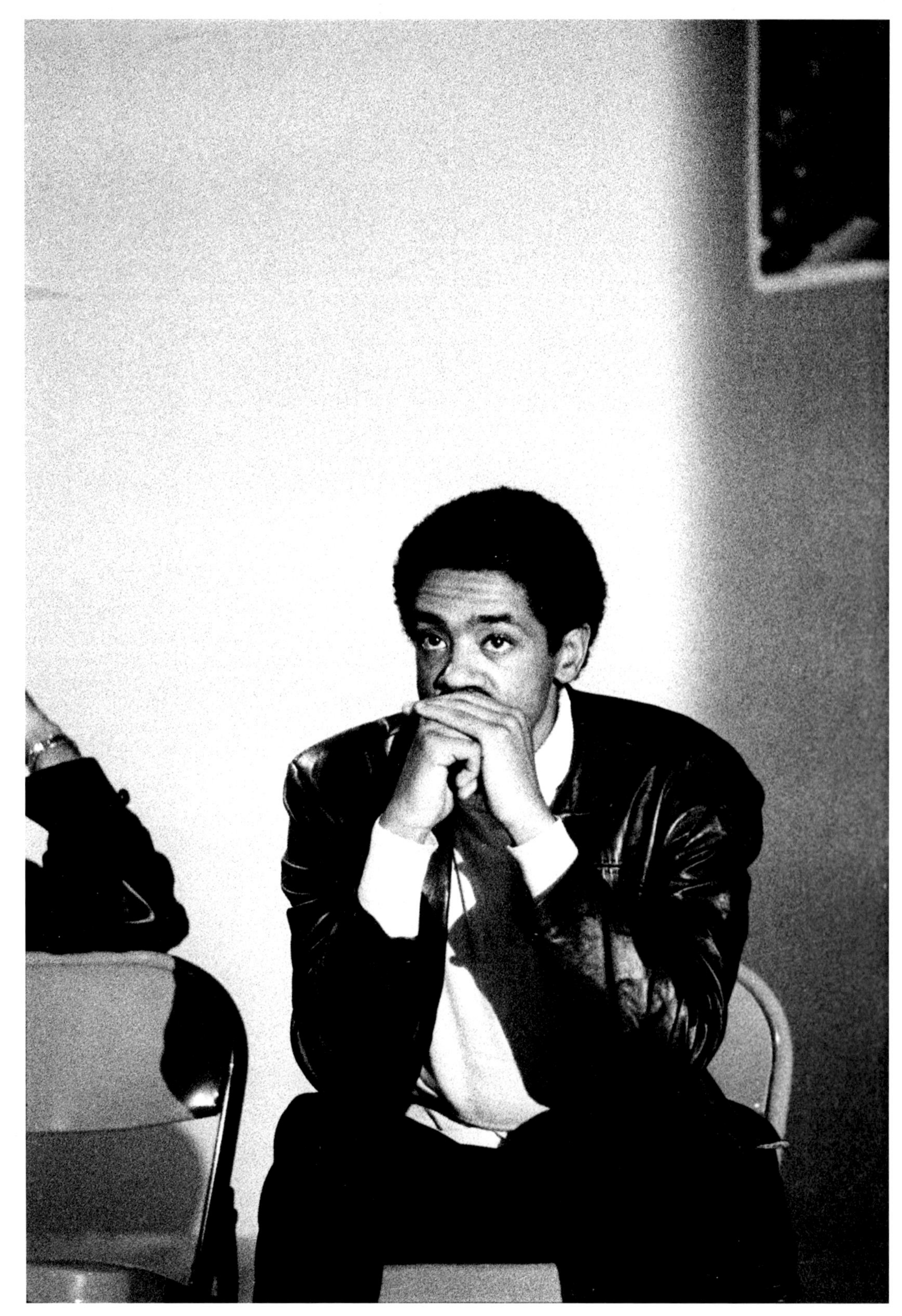

Bobby Seale backstage at a
rally in Marin City, California,
August 22, 1968.

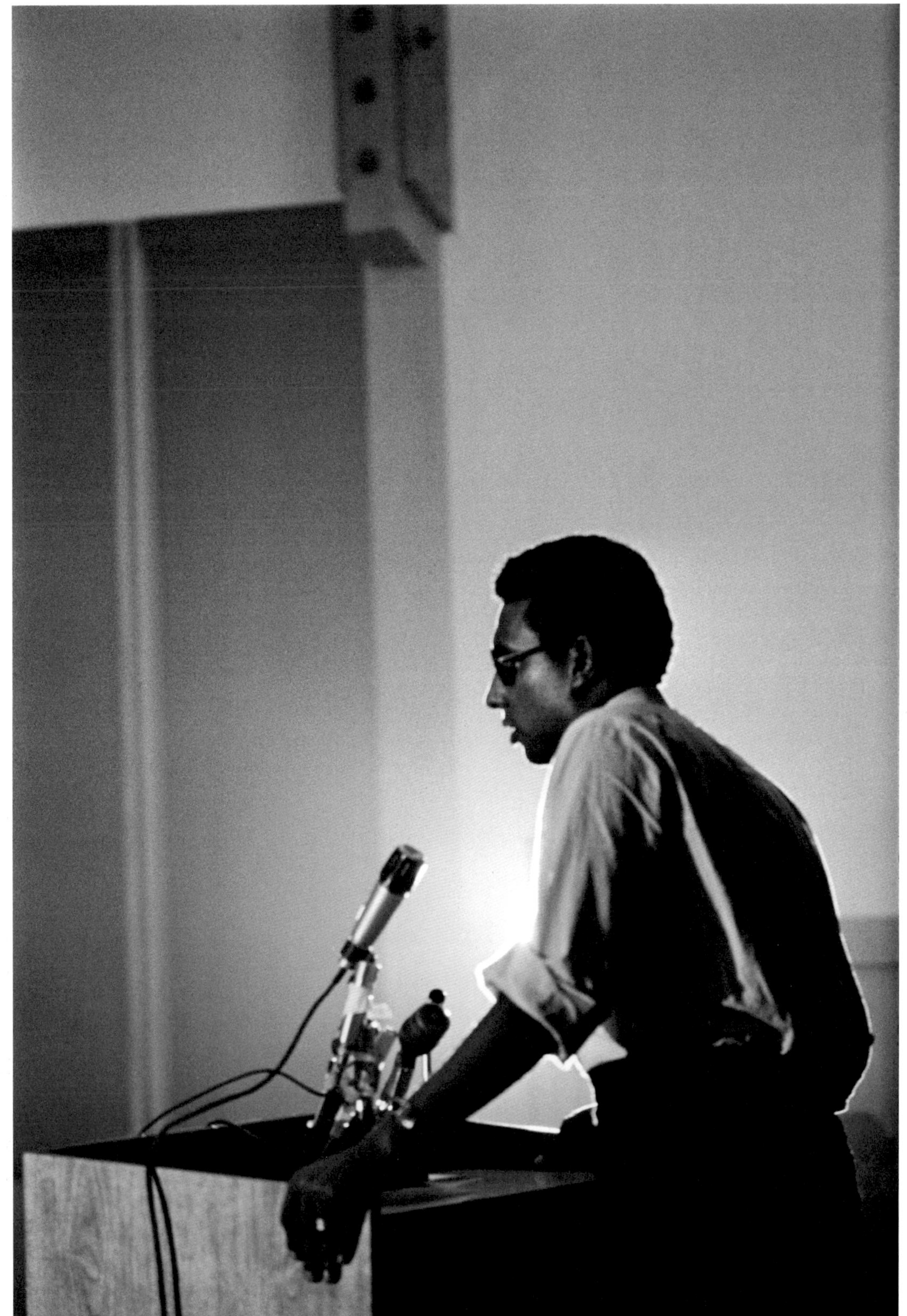

ely Carmichael addressing
Free Huey rally in
in City.

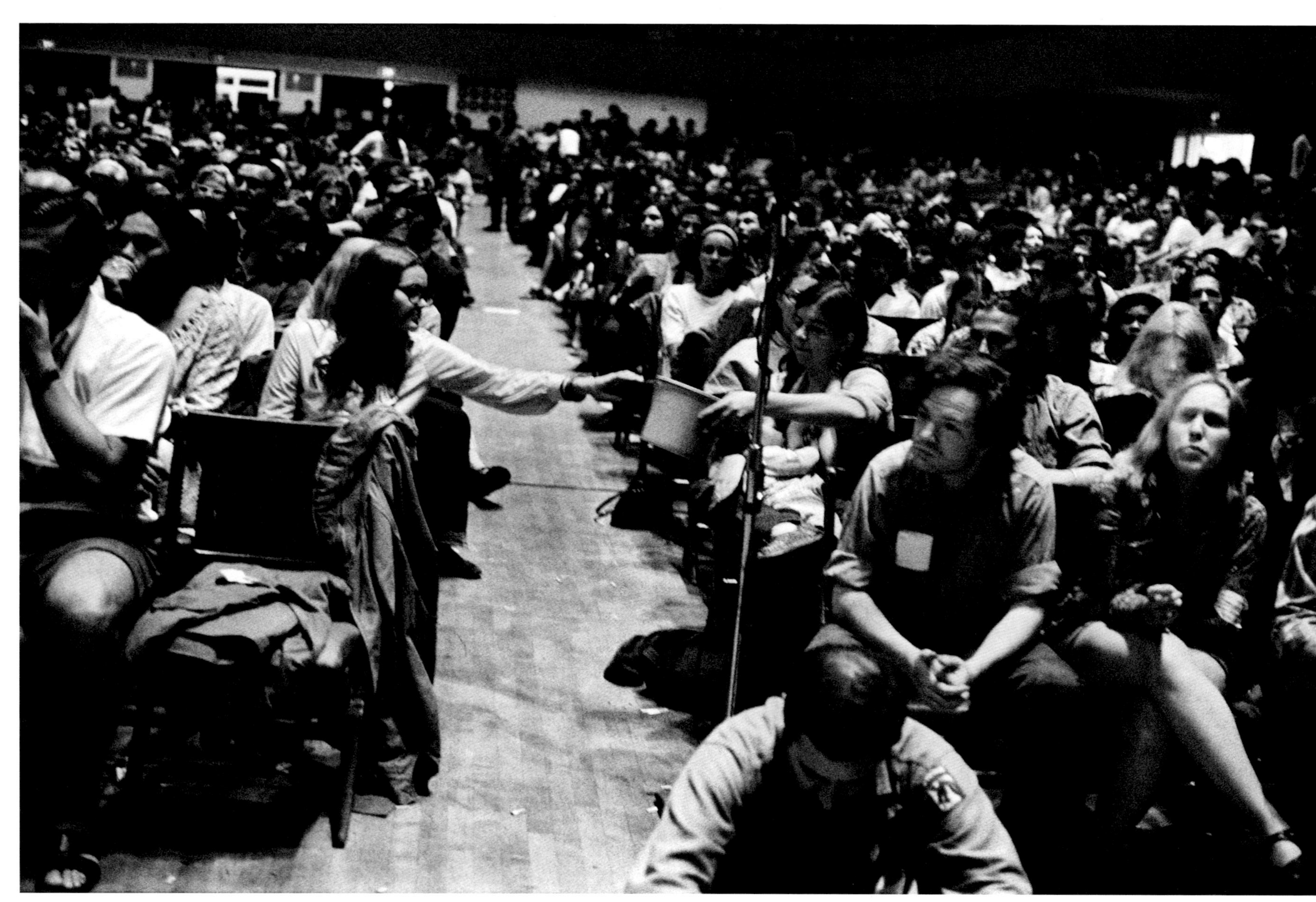

The audience at the Oakland Auditorium during the United Front
Against Fascism conference, July 1969.

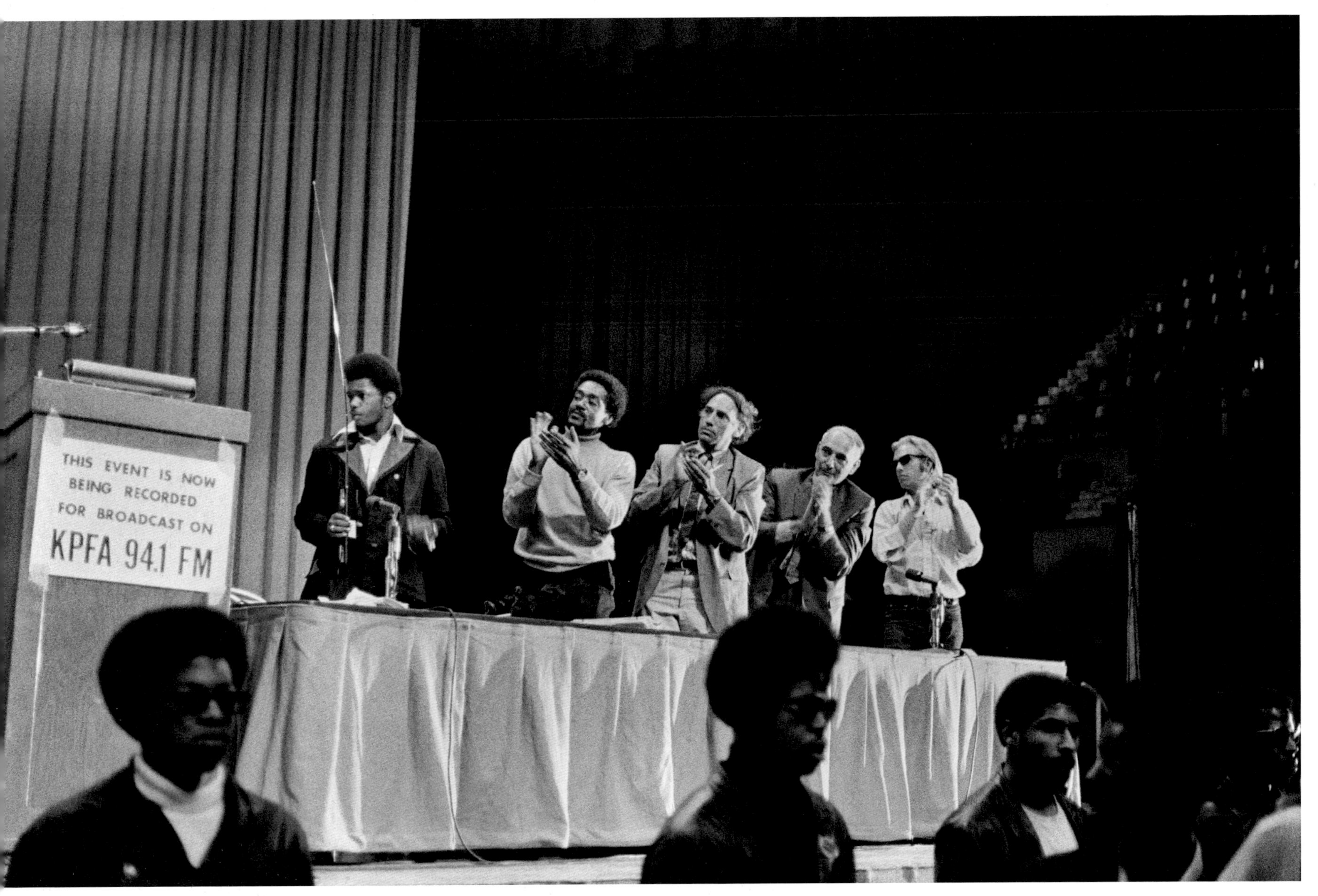



At the 1969 conference, from left: Van Taylor, Bobby Seale, attorneys William Kunstler and Charles Garry, and Jeff Jones, national officer in Students for a Democratic Society (SDS).

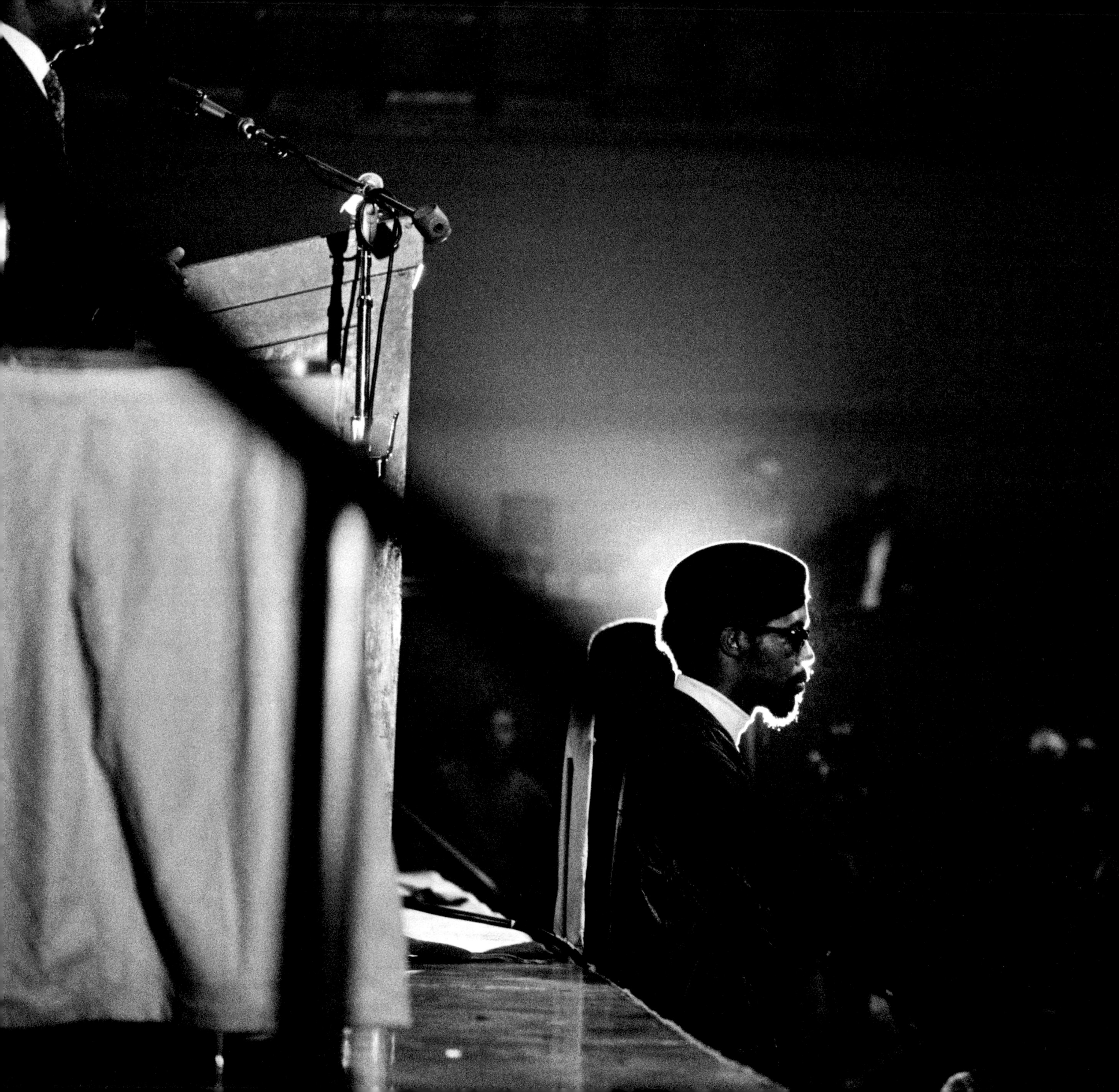

Panther member Randolph Alberry on security at the
Oakland Auditorium, July 1969.

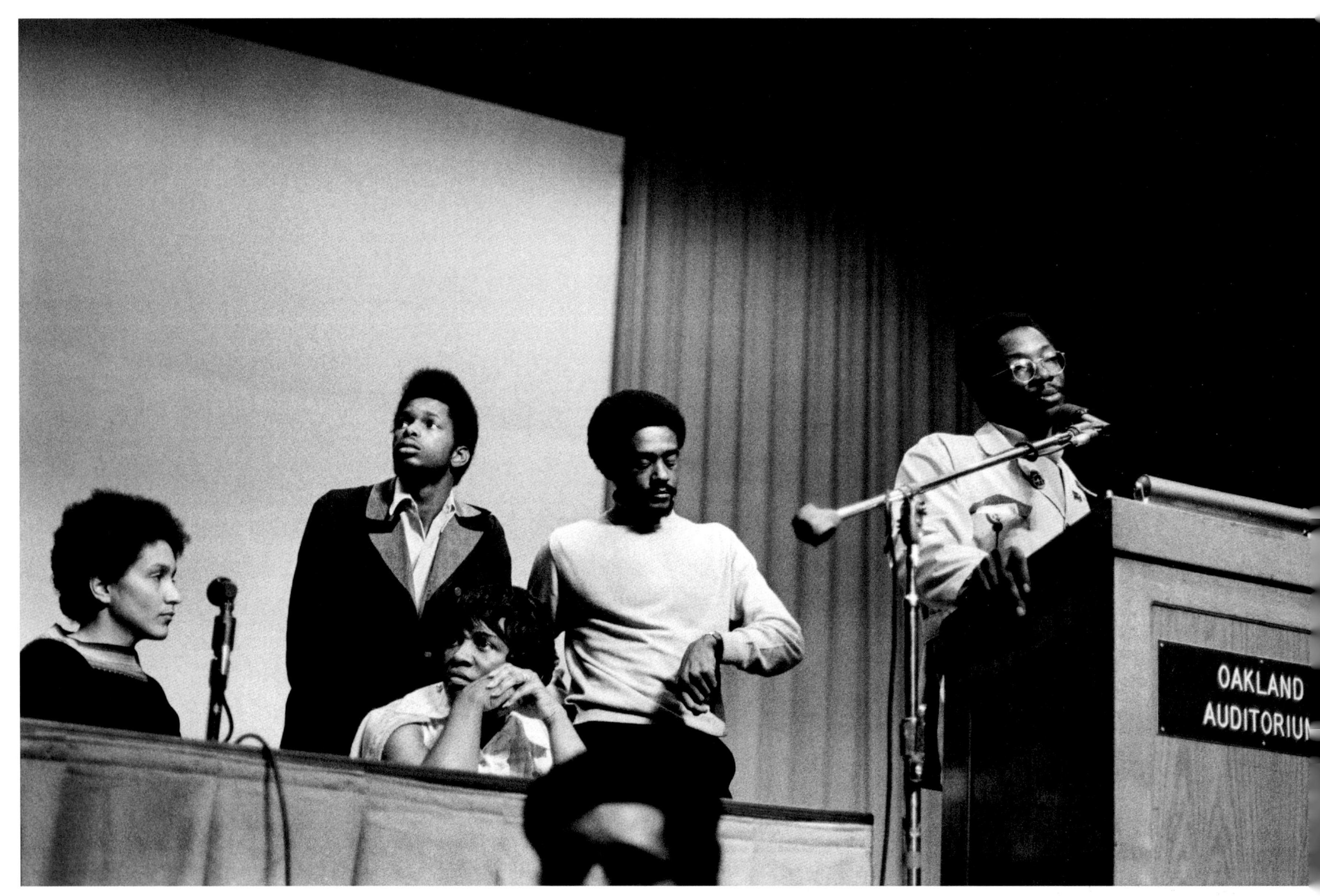

From left: Roberta Alexander, Van Taylor, Evelyn Harris, Bobby Seale and Raymond "Masai" Hewitt, the Panthers' newly appointed Minister of Education, at the conference.

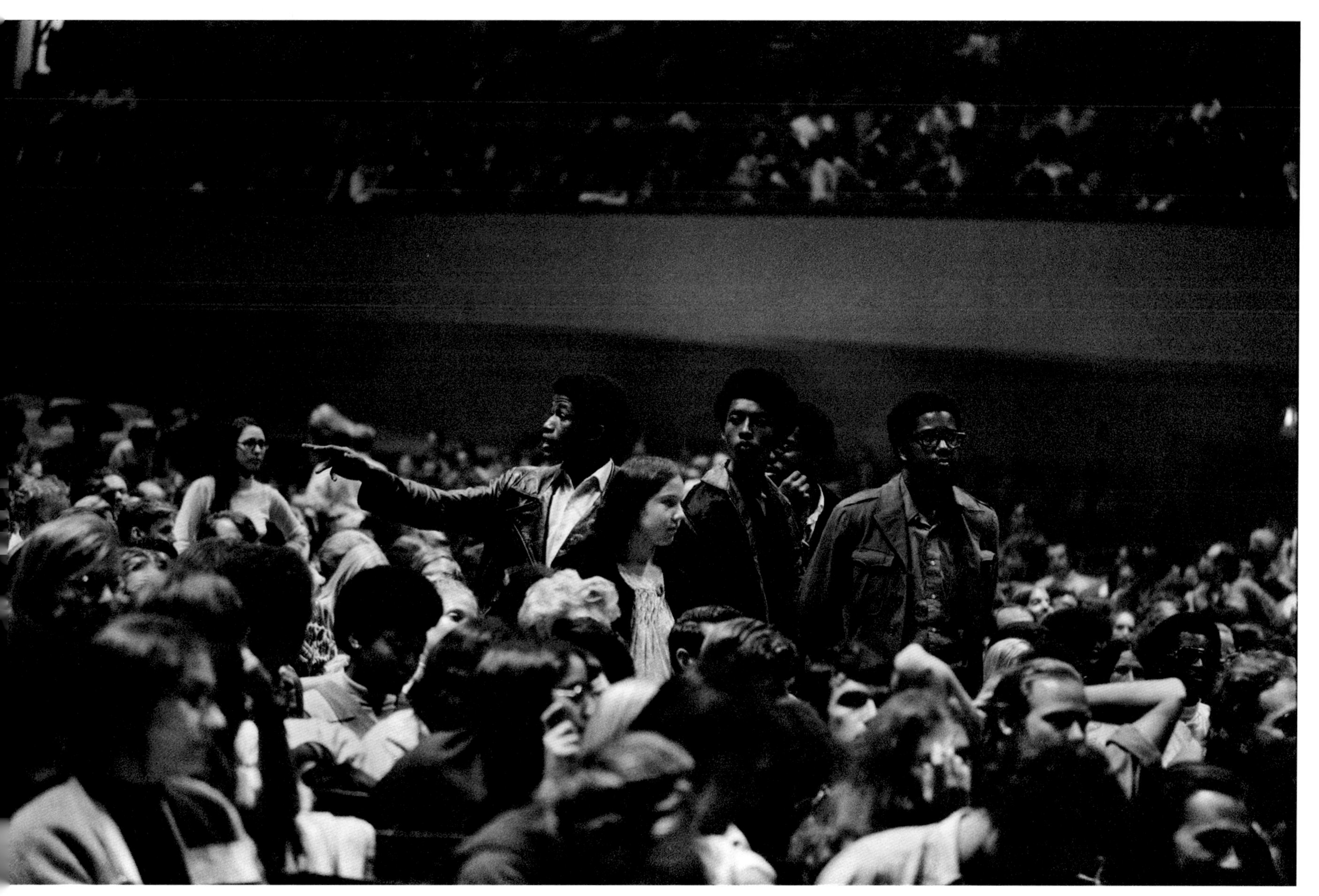

Black Panther Party security at the Oakland Auditorium during the conference.

Black Panther Party Chairman Bobby Seale encouraged me
to contribute to their newspaper, The Black Panther. I would
regularly photograph the organization's events and the civil
unrest at U.C. Berkeley.

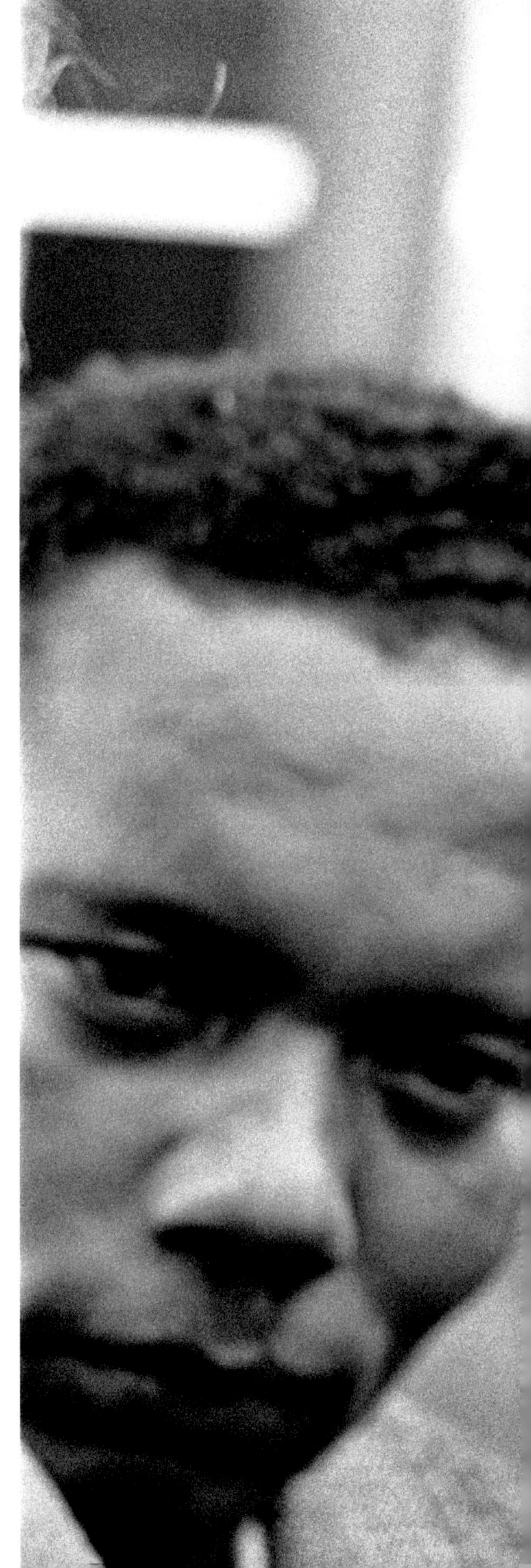

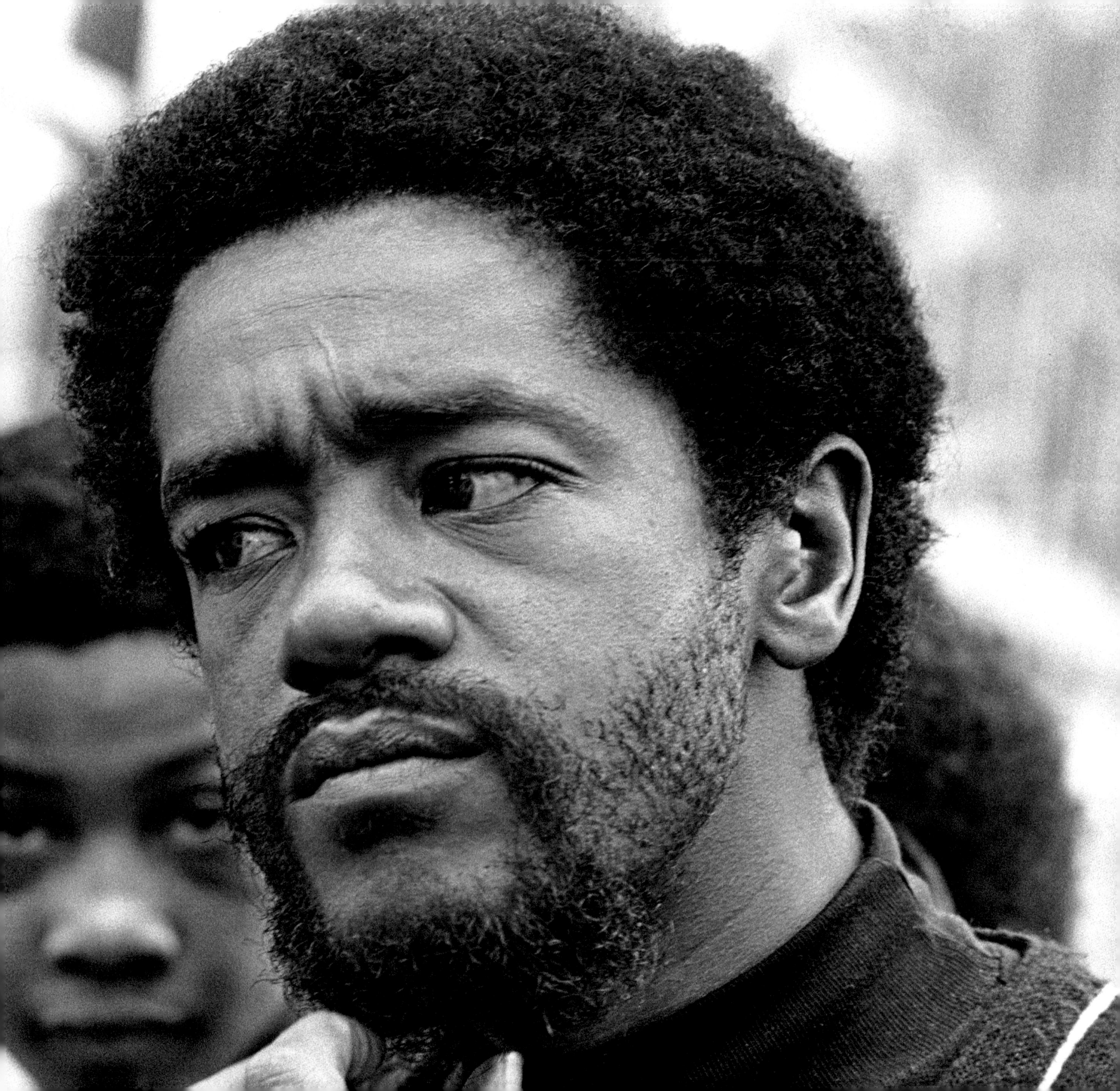

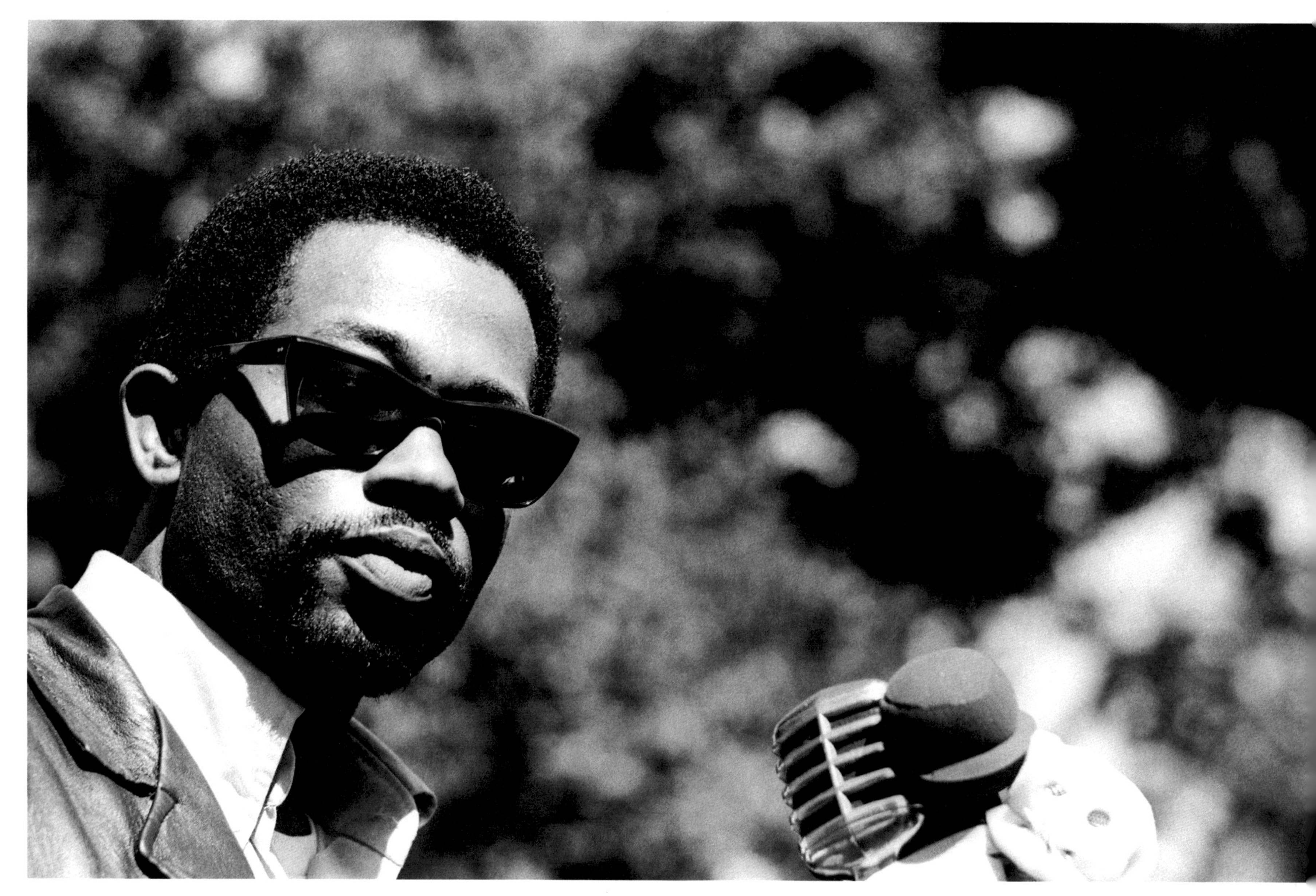

Eldridge Cleaver in DeFremery Park, 196[...]

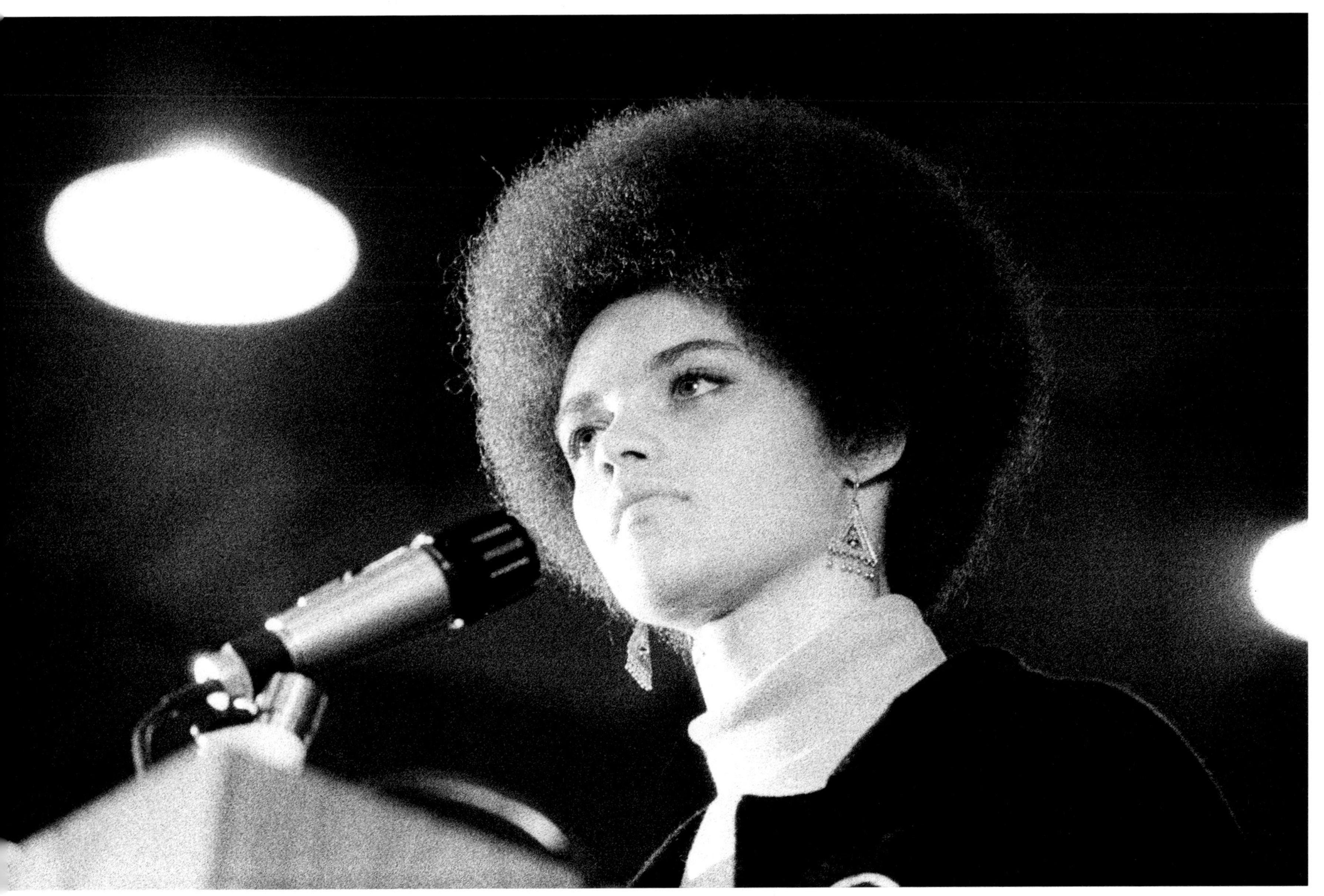

Kathleen Cleaver in Marin City, August 22, 1968.

I'd just turned 16 when I took one of my last photographs of the Black Panthers. Huey Newton held a press conference at the office of his lawyers, Charles Garry and Fay Stender, on August 5,1970, the day he was released from jail after his manslaughter conviction was overturned by the California Court of Appeals. Newton had been in jail for two years.

So much had changed since that fateful October morning in 1967 when a police traffic stop gone bad launched the movement to "Free Huey." It turned the vanguard of the African American civil rights struggle into a global movement focused on police violence and community needs in over-policed and under-served American communities of color.

So much in all of our lives would continue to change, in ways unforeseen to me at the time. Sadly, however, so many of the issues that motivated us during these inspired years of activism in America remain unresolved.

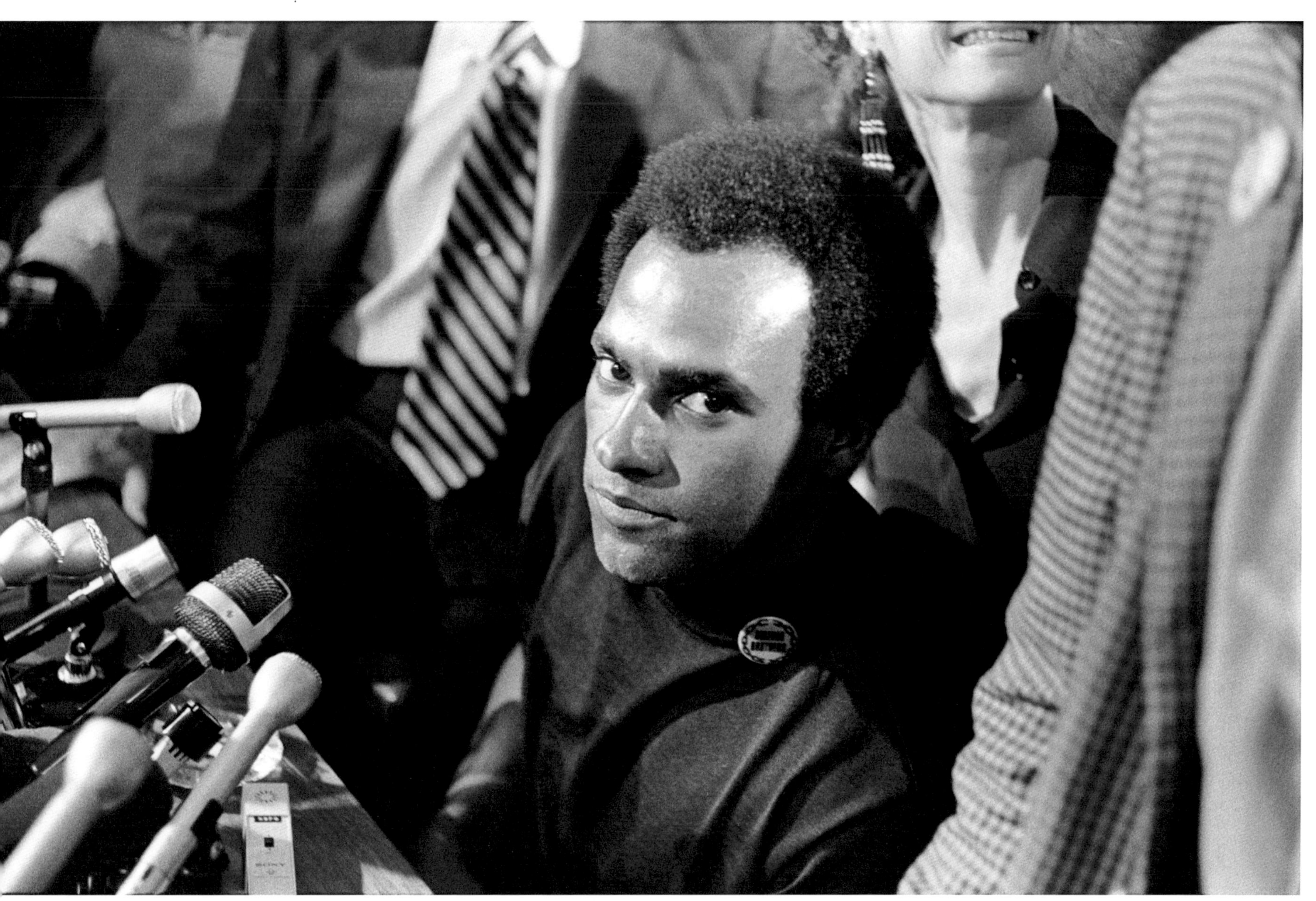

# IN A TIME OF PANTHERS

## BY JEFFREY HENSON SCALES

In 2017, my mother passed away peacefully in Berkeley. When our family was preparing to sell the house, a long-forgotten collection of negative sheets was found: photographs I had made as a teenager during the turbulent 1960s in the San Francisco Bay Area.

With these aged strips of film my mother had tucked away for half a century, fragmented pieces of my memory have been returned to me like broken artifacts that now can be mended back together for display.

The resurfacing of these images not only brings to light the earliest signposts on the path my life would take as a photographer; it also reinforces moments in my memory that deeply affected my sense of right and wrong and my awakening to the need for documentary truth in the pursuit of racial justice.

At our family home in Berkeley's Claremont area, with its spectacular view of the San Francisco Bay, my parents, who were politically active at the time, hosted a grand party in 1967 to celebrate the transition in the SNCC leadership from Stokely Carmichael to H. Rap Brown. In addition to Stokely and Rap Brown, many of the local political elite were there, including Eldridge Cleaver and other members of the Panther Party.

I have never forgotten that night!

I was a middle school kid in Berkeley but drawn to the Haight-Ashbury neighborhood of San Francisco, where we previously lived. One June evening when I was just 12 years old, my parents caught me trying to climb out of the fourth-floor window of our home to go see Jimi Hendrix at the Fillmore Auditorium in San Francisco. It was then they decided it was time for me to spend the summer with my father's sister and her family in Minnesota and travel with my paternal grandmother, Lillian, to meet my relatives in Des Moines, Iowa City, Davenport, Detroit, and Chicago.

But the summer in the Midwest wasn't a bucolic escape from the Bay Area to visit family. On the contrary, it was to become known as The Long Hot Summer of 1967; 159 violent uprisings broke out in Black communities across the country. In the Midwest, I saw for the first time the brutal face of violent repression and  devastation in poor communities of color.

One of our planned destinations was Detroit, where one of the most severe rebellions was taking place. There, 43 people died and hundreds were injured. So we had to detour back to Chicago. It was there that my grandmother gave me a Kodak Instamatic camera, and one of those rolls was part of the collection my mother filed away. For the first time since 1967, I am seeing these and other negatives again.

Old, dusty, and scratched, these are the only record I have of that summer. They were my first photographs in an inner city. That experience shifted my adolescent perspective.

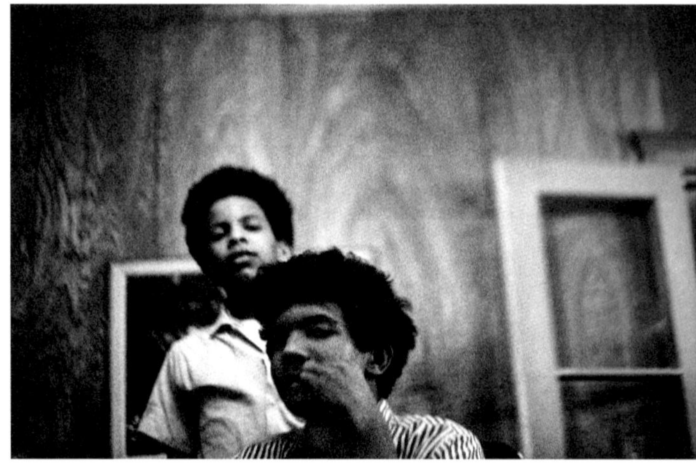
My older brother, Michael, and me, circa 1967.

Returning to Berkeley after that Midwest summer, I was profoundly changed. I felt compelled to document these urban realities, and the activists who were trying to change them. I too wanted to do my part to try to change the world.

By the summer of 1968, protests for civil rights and against the Vietnam War and the draft were flourishing. My younger brother, Fred, was just 3, but older brother Michael, 18, was draft eligible, so he had moved to Canada.

I was entering the ninth grade and not quite 14 years old when I began photographing the Oakland Chapter of the Black Panther Party. It was a most revelatory experience.

The leadership of the Black Panthers took me under their wing and mentored me: I would often visit Huey Newton in jail at the Alameda County Courthouse while he was on trial for murder in the killing of an Oakland police officer during a traffic stop. We talked through a small viewing window framed by walls of thick steel on one of those old-style telephone receivers. Despite having been shot and being on trial for his life, he was always attentive, affable, and full of quick wit.

The Black Panther Party chairman, Bobby Seale, encouraged me to be a photographer for their newspaper, The Black Panther. I would regularly cover the organization's events as well as civil unrest at U.C. Berkeley.

Emory Douglas, the graphic artist who art-directed all the Panthers' imagery as well as their newspaper, was the first to publish my work. It was a graffiti-style painting I had made of Lil' Bobby Hutton that

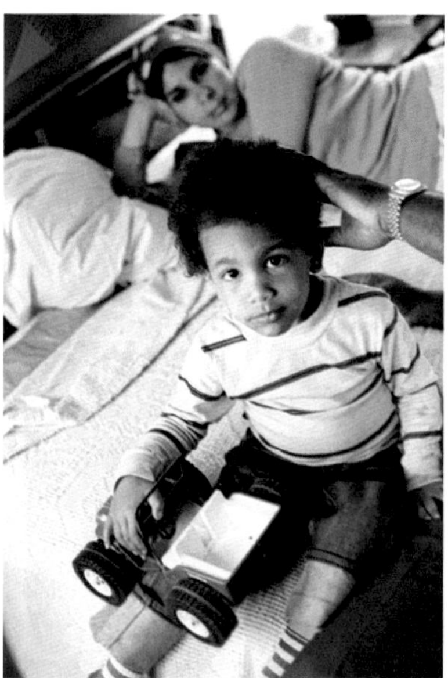
My younger brother, Fred, getting groomed by our parents for his birthday, circa 1968.

Emory put on the cover of the paper after his murder. He even invited me to work on the production of their newspaper at the home of its editor, Eldridge Cleaver, who lived with his wife, Kathleen, in San Francisco.

I first met Cleaver one day when I was hanging out at the Panther office in Oakland, and he'd stopped by. Bobby Seale came over and introduced us. He said, "Eldridge, this is Jeffrey Scales. He's going to be taking photos for the paper."
Cleaver looked at me and asked, "Is Emmet Scales your father?"
"Yeah?" I replied.
"Do you still live in that big house in the Berkeley Hills?"
"Uh, yeah?"
"Tell your dad, y'all need to have a book party for my new book up there!"
"OK, I'll ask him."
And a few weeks later, we had that party.

Some of the photographs I took during that time haunt me more than others. Memories, of course, of those who were killed back in those days, others who may be still imprisoned after decades, or others who have passed on, and some memories of my disappointment in the journeys some of my then-idols made in their later years.

But a few of these images evoke even stronger ghosts:

The Saturday after Dr. Martin Luther King Jr. was assassinated in Memphis, 17-year-old Panther Bobby Hutton was killed by the Oakland police. The morning after, the Panther leadership called me to come down and make some photographs.

Charred debris from the basement where Eldridge and Lil' Bobby had holed up had been dragged out to the street. The smell of burnt wood and the acrid stench of tear gas and gunfire still filled the rooms. Seeing the photographs of that devastation after so many years disturbed me more than I would have imagined. They bring back the feelings I had that day, as an idealistic teenager being confronted with the harsh reality of governmental violence directed at Black activists, just days after the murder of Dr. King.

In 1969, I also made photographs during riots in Berkeley over People's Park, a university-owned lot that people had turned into a park without permission. To stop the occupation, the police used shotguns with buckshot on the crowds, killing one and blinding another.

I was not a protester, just a teenager with a camera. I was with some protesters on the balcony of one of the buildings on the U.C. Berkeley campus when two officers, one with a standard 12-gauge pump-action shotgun and the other with a tear-gas canister launching shotgun, approached on the street below us. The officer with the shotgun looked up at us and shouldered his weapon to fire. I knew it was time to take cover. In what in memory seems like slow motion, the shots rang out at us, buckshot splattering on the pillars we had hidden behind, followed by his partner firing a tear gas grenade onto the balcony where we stood.

The second time that day I was shot at, I literally dodged a bullet. I was at street level when a group of

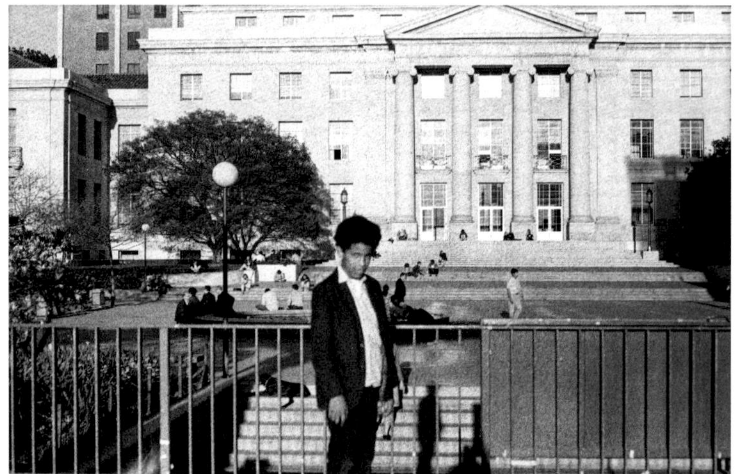

As a teenager in Berkeley, I was often on the university campus.

police officers rounded the corner, chasing and beating all the demonstrators in their path with nightsticks, when one with a shotgun came after me.

I noticed a narrow alley and fled. Running faster than I ever had, and certainly ever since, I saw what looked like a 12-foot concrete wall dead-ending my escape route. I suspect the wall was far shorter than that, but it presented what felt like a potentially deadly obstacle.

I quite literally took a leap of faith and propelled myself as forcefully and as quickly as I could to the top of the wall. As I dropped over to the other side, I heard a

shotgun blast ring out, echoing off the alley walls, like deadly thunder just a few meters behind me.

I didn't look back and proceeded as fast as I could, as far as my legs and the air in my lungs would take me before looking back and seeing that I had safely escaped. With the arrival of 2,700 National Guard troops overnight, Berkeley became an occupied city.

This past has now come back to confront me more than 50 years on, in this new century in America.
Because of chance circumstance, during a sharply focused arc of American history that seemed to unfold around me when I was merely a child, much of this past not only belongs to my memory but also is one that has been fixed into our collective American psyche.

Yet these memories of struggle have been returned to me at a time where there are powerful forces trying to push the clock back, to the time before these photographs were made. It's a desperate effort to reverse the progress America has made since that sharp arc of history helped form our contemporary and somewhat more inclusive American identity.

# ACKNOWLEDGMENTS

This book is dedicated to my parents, Emmet T. Scales Jr. and Barbara Jean Scales, née Hadsall.

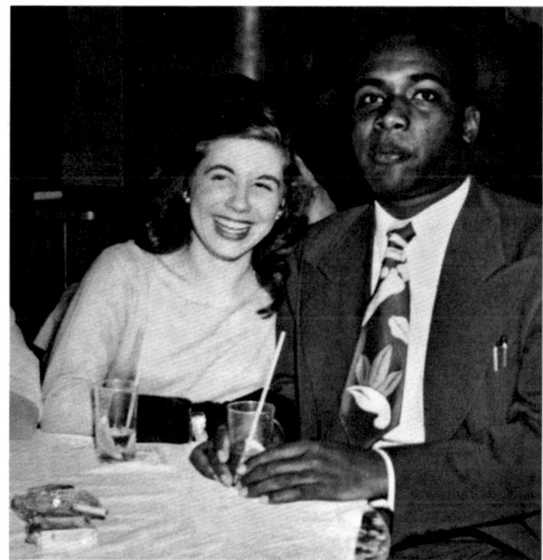

Barbara and Emmet, 1949.

They fell in love in Iowa in the 1940's, moved out west and made a family in which creating art, love, freedom and work were the principles they raised their children with — the principles that have carried me throughout my life.

Thank you to:

Keith Alward, for decades of love and continuing efforts that have kept us all family. My brothers, Michael and Fred, for always being there and taking care of business and family. My wife, Meg Henson Scales, for her unconditional love and patience with me and this project. My daughter, Coco, for being such a fantastic, inspiring human and parent to our granddaughter, Charly.

The courageous men and women in these images who mentored, educated, encouraged, and entitled me with the remarkable access that inspired me to begin this lifelong photographic journey: Bobby Seale, Eldridge Cleaver, Emory Douglass, Huey Newton, David Hilliard, Kathleen Cleaver and Stephen Shames.

Tom and Anna at SPQR for their enthusiasm and commitment, and their guidance in the structuring, design and producing of this book, including the decades of support they have always given for my work. Deborah and Waldo for the great essays. Trish Hall for editing the texts and Sandy Byers Harvin for copyediting everything. Tazewell Thompson for additional edits, as well as his encouragement and guidance in the telling of my story. Robbin Schiff for scrutinizing what we put on the pages. Billy X Jennings and Ericka Huggins for their fact checking and advice. The photography staff at The New York Times for their encouragement and support, particularly William O'Donnell for his digital image scanning and restoration. Rebecca Pietri for helping me frame what's happening in the 21st century, as well as Shina Peng and Ryan Walker for keeping the archive project running.

Claire and Ian of The Claire Oliver Gallery for all they do to get my work out into the world and their efforts that helped make this book even possible. Eli Keneally and Kevin McCarthy and the team at Griffin Editions for the great exhibition prints and additional production.

And finally let us never forget to salute the people who gave their lives in this struggle, as well as remember there are those who remain imprisoned as a result of their activism, still paying a price for fighting for racial and social justice in this country.

Book: ©2022 SPQR Editions, LLC · Photographs: ©2022 Jeffrey Henson Scales
Texts: ©2022 Deborah Willis · ©2022 Waldo E. Martin Jr.
All rights reserved.



Published in the United States by SPQR Editions LLC, Brooklyn, NY
Website: spqreditions.com
Library of Congress Control Number: 2022937640
Hardcover ISBN: 978-1648230233
Printed and bound in Italy by INDUSTRIA GRAFICA SI.Z. Verona
First edition, 2022
Editing and sequencing by Thomas Roma
Design and production by Anna Roma
10 9 8 7 6 5 4 3 2 1

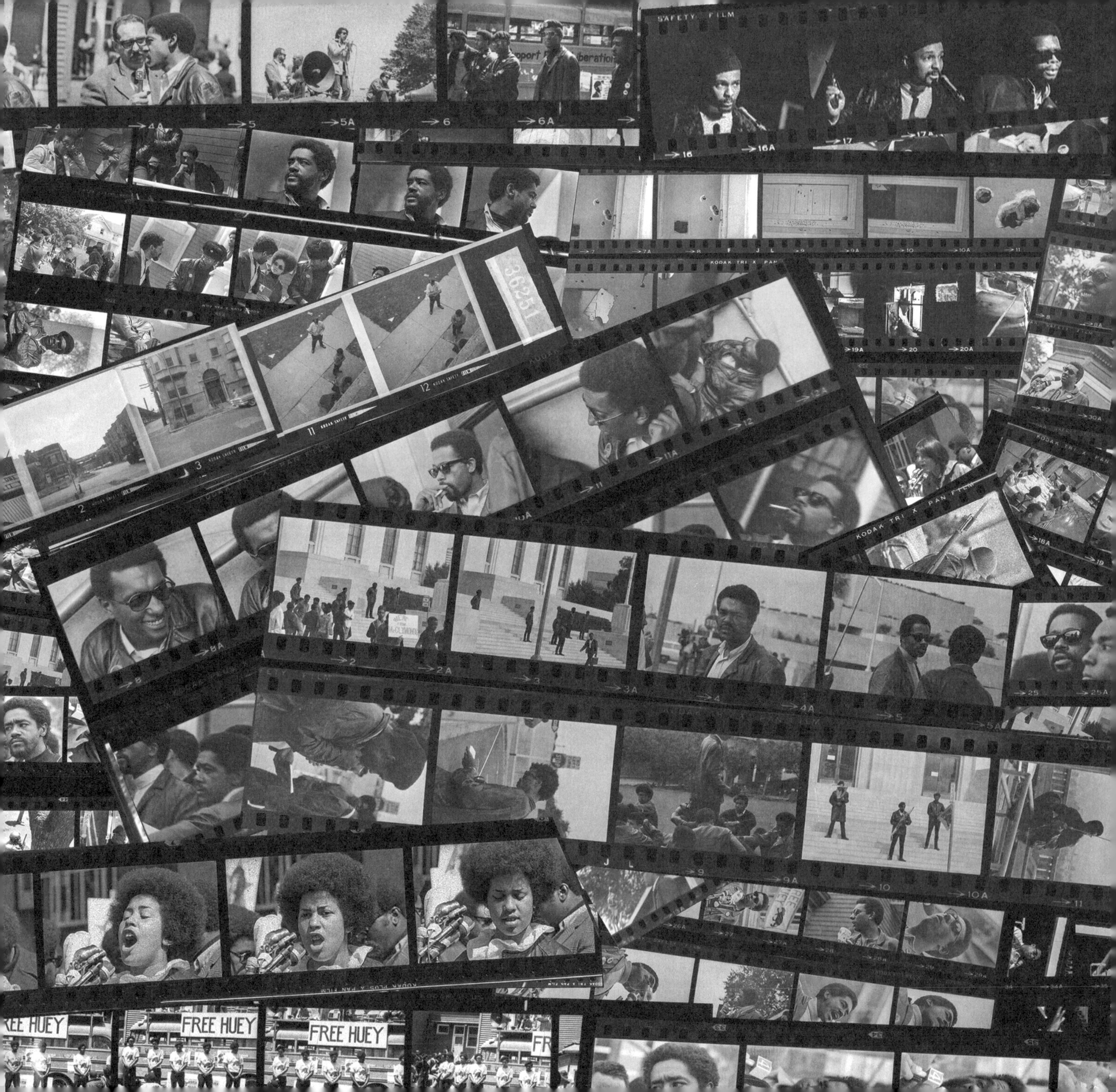